The Best
Men's Stage Monologues
of 2007

The Best
Men's Stage Monologues
of 2007

edited by Lawrence Harbison
foreword by D. L. Lepidus

MONOLOGUE AUDITION SERIES

A SMITH AND KRAUS BOOK

Published by Smith and Kraus, Inc.
177 Lyme Road, Hanover, NH 03755
www.SmithandKraus.com

© 2008 by Smith and Kraus, Inc.
All rights reserved
Manufactured in the United States of America

First Edition: January 2008
10 9 8 7 6 5 4 3 2 1

Cover illustration: *Box Seats* by Lisa Goldfinger
Cover and text design and production by Julia Hill Gignoux

The Monologue Audition Series
ISSN 1067-134X
ISBN 978-1-57525-586-6

Library of Congress Control Number: 2007939331

NOTE: These monologues are intended to be used for audition and class study; permission is not required to use the material for those purposes. However, if there is a paid performance of any of the monologues included in this book, please refer to the Rights and Permissions pages 96-100 to locate the source that can grant permission for public performance.

CONTENTS

FOREWORD

In these pages, you will find a rich and varied selection of monologues from recent plays, almost all of which have been published. They are thus readily available to you when you have found that perfect monologue to work on in class or to use for auditions. Many are for younger performers (teens through thirties), but there are also some excellent pieces for men in their forties and fifties, and even a few for older performers. Many are comic (laughs), many are dramatic (generally, no laughs). Some are rather short, some are rather long. All represent the best in contemporary playwriting.

Many of the playwrights whose work appears here may be familiar to you — such as Lee Blessing, Terrence McNally, Neal Bell, Arlene Hutton, and Stephen Belber, all of whom have had their work produced On and/or Off Broadway; but you will also find some exciting new voices, up-and-comers like Anna Ziegler, Kathryn Walat, Carlos Murillo, Jeff Goode, Jeff Cohen, and Trish Harnetiaux.

After seven years of doing these books for Smith and Kraus, I have decided to step aside and have turned over the reins to my old pal Lawrence Harbison, who knows as much about the theater and its plays and playwrights as anyone I know. It has been a very rewarding and very challenging task editing these anthologies, but now it is time to hang up my red pencil. I am retiring to Myrtle Beach, there to become one of those geezers who stands around all day in a kilt, sending foursomes of awful golfers off the first tee. In my free time I won't be reading plays: I'll be taking up bungee jumping, hang gliding, and allligator wrestling. There is life beyond the theater.

Break a leg.

— D.L. Lepidus, Editor
Brooklyn, N.Y.

ASYLUM
Keith Aisner

Dramatic
Salesman, late twenties to early thirties

The Salesman is talking to Gary, who is spiraling out of control. Gary is about to take a sleeping pill to try and regain his mental stability. The Salesman is the personification of all his fears.

SALESMAN: Words, Gary? You want me to use words to tell you the meaning of your own soul? Would you like to buy a goddamned vowel?
. . . It doesn't work like that, Gary. You stop now and, if you're lucky, you'll have to start all over again from square one. And then what? You'll just try again? Next time? Why are you so sure there's going to be a next time? What, you think you'll just be able to swan dive into this very rare form of perception again, no problemo? C'mon. Who knows how close to me, your guide, your friend, you might make it the next time you try, if you make it at all? And that's supposing that right now you can actually paddle all the way up to the surface from the murky depths in which you are currently swimming without getting a mental case of the bends. I mean, give it some thought, cowboy. You've been bruisin' the old bean there. And I'll tell you something. I'll tell you what everyone else knows but hasn't told you. All that fuckin' around you've been doin' inside your head? There's a real good chance you did some damage. Serious, permanent damage. I'm talking collecting early Social Security on a regular-type-basis damage. Alright? You see? You're already too invested. You made it this far. You are so goddamned close . . . inches, man . . . just inches. And now you're going to give up? Throw it all away. Just because some people think they know what they're talking about; people who, may I remind you, have never set foot in this land you so easily stride through, people who want you . . . to give up. Be a man. Do this for you. Take the pills and throw them in the sink and we'll finish this tonight; we'll see it through. You and me.

BACK OF THE THROAT
Yussef El Guindi

Dramatic
Carl, could be any age. Probably, thirties to forties

> *Carl, a government agent, is convinced that Khaled, an Arab-American writer, is somehow involved with terrorist cells inside the United States. Here he is using strong-arm tactics to interrogate him.*

CARL: You really give a bad name to immigrants, you know that. Because of you we have to pass tougher laws that stop people who might actually be good for us.

. . . God: I know your type, so well. The smiling little Semite who gives you one face while trying to stab you with the other. You're pathetic, you know that. If you hate us, then just hate us. But you don't have the balls to do even that. You bitch and you moan and complain how overrun you are by us and all the time you can't wait to get here. You'd kill for a visa. That pisses me off. That's hypocrisy. Why not just come clean and own up that you hate everything this country stands for.

. . . No, that's right, because you're too busy envying us.

. . . I could snap your neck just for that. What's the expression for "fuck-face" in Arabic? "Hitit khara"? "Sharmoot"?

. . . Just how crushed do you feel, Khaled? *(Slight beat, then:)* All right, I'm done. *(He lets go and stands up. Beat.)* Now do you want to tell me what you and Asfoor got up to in the strip club? Were you passing a message on to him? Were you the Internet guy? The guy to help him get around? A carrier for something? What? What? Tell me, or I'll — *(Carl pulls his foot back as if to kick him.)*

. . . I'll exercise my drop kick on your testicle sac and make you sing an Arabic song in a very unnatural key.

. . . You're going to be sick. I'm the one who's throwing up. Only I have the decency to do it quietly, inside, and not make a public spectacle of myself. *(Perhaps grabbing Khaled by his lapels.)* What did he want from you? What did he want? What fucked-up part did you play in all of this? What happened with you in there? What happened when you met up with Asfoor? What did he want? . . . You know what I really resent? . . . What you force us to become. To protect ourselves. We are a decent bunch and do not want to be dragged down to your level. But no, you just have to drag us down, don't you. You have to gross us out with your level of crap. I personally hate this, you know that. I hate it when I have to beat the shit out of someone because then by an act of willful horror, whose effect on my soul I can only imagine, I have to shut out everything good about me to do my job to defend and protect. Here I am quickly devolving into a set of clichés I can barely stomach and you have the nerve to think you can vomit. No, it is I who am throwing up, sir, and if I see one scrap of food leave your mouth I will shove it back so far down your throat you'll be shitting it before you even know what you've swallowed again.

BEL CANTO
Reneé Flemings

Dramatic
Trigger, mid-thirties to late forties

> *Trigger, an assassin for hire, is talking to Mains, who has been assigned to carry out a hit on an opposing gang's leader. Mains has asked him how he felt about the first murder he ever committed.*

TRIGGER: Had a steak. About this thick, with potatoes, some bourbon, good bourbon. See, my first was up close. Guy sitting right across from me in this bar. I coulda waited 'til his back was turned. We coulda taken him out in the car and blam, right in the back of the head. But I didn't wanna go like that. I figure you take a man out, he's got a right to see you — to look you in the eye. Right? So, I met him for a drink in this little joint in Brooklyn, it was set up lovely, real lovely. The bartender was the only one there besides us. He knew what was goin' on and he knew when it was time. He just walked into the back room, closed the door. Jinx, the guy not the bartender, the guy. Jinx took a sip of this little fruity drink he had, a margarita I think, some shit like that. There was this thick line of salt all around the rim of the glass, looked like sugar . . . I could see lights dancing around in the glass, all kinds of colors — from the neon outside . . . Dizzy was on the jukebox "Salt Peanuts, salt peanuts" yeah — anyway so he takes a sip, looks me dead in the eye and says: "So? What you want to talk about?" I didn't say a word. I just looked at him for a long, long minute — I think he knew it was coming. He knew. Blam. All over. Then I sat there for, I don't know, a minute, maybe two and I started gettin' this gnawing feeling in my stomach — like I had a hole in me. I remember looking down at that glass, there was a few little specks of blood on it . . . But all that salt, all that salt around the rim was pink now . . . Pink and wet. I'm lookin' at that salt thinkin' "pink and wet" . . . Like meat, you now? Good meat. I got in the car. Drove down to Dane's joint and had me the biggest cut of beef I ever had.

BFF
Anna Ziegler

Dramatic
Seth, twenties

Seth is on the phone to his probably ex-girlfriend, who has dumped him for reasons that escape him. He knows her as Eliza. Her true name is Lauren. Here, he is pleading for another chance to make their relationship work.

SETH: Eliza, please pick up the phone. Please. I'm sorry I left you alone. I guess when people say they want to be alone what they really mean is they want to be with other people and I read that all wrong. Please pick up. I mean, I went out with some friends last night and Trevor told this story about a date he had. He met this girl online. Apparently they match perfectly in terms of goals and lifestyle, whatever that means. He says I should go online too, Liza. Meet someone. I say I'm already taken. At that point, my friends all laugh. They shoot each other knowing glances. They say, "Seth, you're a real romantic, aren't you"; they say I went on a few dates and now I think I'm married. And considering the fact that I haven't heard from you, maybe they're right that I thought we were . . . closer than we were. So given all that I've made a sort of promise to myself. I say sort of because it might be hard to stick to but I think I should and so does Nancy — my therapist, I mean. She thinks, and I mean, I agree, that this should be the last message I leave you. It's a very one-sided relationship I'm engaged in, she says, and I guess she's right. So when I hang up I'm not calling back. I mean, I'll call back if you call me first and leave a message. I'm just not going to leave any more of these . . . whatever these are. But before I go . . . I just want to say . . . well, maybe this is my last chance, so why the hell not, right? I mean, I think I was starting to . . . I mean, you might not know it, but I'm not a real hotshot with women; I don't date that much. But I've dated enough . . . I mean, I've met enough women to know that you're really very . . . I mean, I think you're something. Really something. And for what it's worth, whatever it is you're going through right now . . . we can get through it. It'll be OK. I mean I *know* in my gut that if we're together, we can . . . But anyway I guess I'll leave it there. So, well, good-bye. I'm hanging up now. And I won't beg you to call me back . . . but why not just call me back?

BLOOD ORANGE
David Wiener

Dramatic
Ray-Ray, seventeen

> *Ray-Ray is working on Clinton's car. Clinton is an older boy who*
> *has been his tormentor. Clinton is leaving for Mexico, but Ray-Ray*
> *wants him instead to go over to his house to help with his dead*
> *mother. Here, Ray-Ray has just flipped the jack, trapping Clinton*
> *under his car.*

RAY-RAY: Shhh . . . It's all right. Everything's broken now Clinton. I see it
in the sidewalk. That's where it shows. 'Cause of the heat. The way
it makes everything push against everything. It cracks. The concrete.
Where we put our hands. It's all broken. *(Clinton's leg kicks again.)*
Shhh. Don't. Don't. It's all right. I know how it is. Something push
down on you so hard that you can't even breathe. Can't get air to cry
out. To cry. Don't cry. Let's just be quiet now. I feel the part of you
that trickled down my throat. I feel it here. This is where it grows.
It hurts. I got you inside me. Like you said. And you got me. And
we know what each other is and who eats who, right? And we don't
fucking cry. *(Clinton's foot moves. Ray-Ray kneels and looks under the
car.)* It's all right now. You just be quiet. It's your head see. It's got
the wrong shape. Your fucking eye came out Clinton. Came right out
of your head. And your ribs popped loose. And there's bubbles. You
remember when you skinned your knee on the drive? Just a little boy
crying over your knee and it was skinned so bad there wasn't even
blood, just that new white-white skin underneath. Your mom took
you inside. And there was your skin on the driveway right next to
me. You remember that? I touched it. It was all spongy and warm
like it was still a part of you and alive. And I touched it and I wanted
to know what you looked like inside. 'Cause inside, I knew you were
the same color as me. We're the same. I crushed a widow once. It left
blood and black shit all over the back of my trowel. So that's how I

knew what color we were. You're black inside Clinton. I'm black inside. I can see it now. I guess. It looks black. I don't know. Maybe that's just the oil. I can't tell. It's dark underneath. And I can't tell if it's blood or if it's oil Clinton. I can't tell the oil from the blood.

CAROL MULRONEY
Stephen Belber

Dramatic
Ken, thirty-two, black

> *Ken is a control freak but a romantic at heart. In this direct address to the audience, he is talking about his friend Carol, who has recently died.*

KEN: I've always been a huge admirer of sadness; of sad people; of people who don't understand something very . . . vital. *(Beat.)* We live in a world where sadness is devalued, where sad people are considered . . . incompetent. And maybe we are, for there are many ways to be happy and you'd think that we would just embrace one, but . . . *(Beat.)* Carol had sadness running through her veins like bad blood. Consequently, I was drawn to her immediately. I dunno. I just wanna love them; the sad people; people like Carol. I just want to love. Because it's what I'm good at — maybe the only thing I have, this skill of love — this skill *to* love. I love to love. I do. I love it. *(Pause.)* The problem is that the world tends not to love me back. Which makes me very sad. *(Pause.)* And it's a great disappointment because it should; the world, or certain people in it, they *should* love me back. And I get so mad at them when they don't. Because I know I know how to solve them, to help *solve* their sadness. But it's like at some point they just stop listening; like they get too close to the edge . . . and they lose their ability to focus. *(Almost whispering.)* And I get so angry . . . that this beautiful, sad person standing in front of me can't see how much potential happiness I'm offering them. *(Pause.)* It's like . . . "Why can't you just be fucking happy?" *(Pause.)* When of course I already know the answer. Which is that sometimes you just miss the train.

CAROL MULRONEY
Stephen Belber

Dramatic
Lesley, late thirties

> *Lesley is talking to his wife, Carol, about what his job means to him,
> and why she should come down from the roof.*

LESLEY: *(Pause.)* The job is who I am, Carol. It's what I do, it fulfills me
and I need you to respect that.

    . . . — but it's fiscal, right? — it's a fiscal thing, and what *I'm*
talking about is spiritual, is you and I understanding each other in a
whole new way, so that me working for your father becomes irrele-
vant. *(Slower, more tender.)* Because listen to me, it doesn't matter what
you do, what matters is that the spirit inside of you is alive, and that
you go to bed each night knowing in your gut that nothing is un-
surmountable, that no problem is answerless as long as you set a goal
for tomorrow that no one can talk you out of. *(Genuine, even tender,
as he brushes away her hair.)* You can live in Zimbabwe or on this
roof — it doesn't matter. You just have to know that inside you there
are solutions. And I'll help you find 'em but you have to be with me.
You have to want it just as bad . . . I'm serious. I've never been more
serious in my life! But, you have to trust me. *(Pause; honest.)* Will
you try?

CAROL MULRONEY
Stephen Belber

Dramatic
Lesley, late thirties

> *In this direct address to the audience, Lesley is talking about what his wife Carol meant to him. Carol has recently jumped off the roof.*

LESLEY: I believe in God. *(Beat.)* I believe God guides us. That He takes us to the mountain . . . and then He shows us the pit of hell. I really do believe that. *(Beat.)* Consequently, I wonder where God will have guided me twenty years from now. I wonder if I'll wake up each day and reach for Carol's picture on my bedside table — next to my breath mints and unused condoms — and hold this faded photo, and weep and mutter to myself that "this woman is the only reason I ever had for getting out of bed." *(Pause.)* And I'm wondering if this thought is what God will have given me to get me through the day. But the thing is, I might not even *own* her picture. I might be married to someone else, more my "type," the type who's simple and knowable and wears bright red dresses on dark cloudy days. And maybe I won't need the thought of Carol to get me through the day. *(Beat.)* Who knows. God works in mysterious ways. *(Beat . . .)* I guess what I choose to believe . . . is that Carol was OK. That she finally and fully understood something, when she closed her eyes and fell. When she flew towards her answer through the sparkling night sky. I prefer to believe that she'd glimpsed a truth; that some force from above became momentarily gracious and descended from the sky, and in its descent it became visible to Carol, and this descent she recognized as beauty. I prefer to believe that she decided to grab hold of this beauty; and thus she fell . . . in order to ascend. *(Pause.)* That might not be true, but it's what I believe.

11

DARK PLAY;
OR STORIES FOR BOYS
Carlos Murillo

Dramatic
Nick, late teens, early twenties

> *Nick has just had sex with a new girlfriend. This is direct address
> to the audience.*

NICK: I make shit up.

> I make shit up all the time
> partly cause I like making shit up
> partly cause I'm good at it
> and partly cause
> well
> I *can.*
> Which is not to say that I'm oblivious to the consequences
> Christ, do I know there are consequences.
> You find yourself in sticky situations, painted into corners
> And it takes the dexterity of a sharp-thinking comic book hero
> to
> *Unstick* yourself, tiptoe across the wet paint
> Hoping you don't leave a trail of painted toe prints,
> Or if you do,
> that they're faint enough so no one will notice.
>
> I'm thinking about this right now
> Cause
> Well
> I find myself in one of those sticky situations
> Situation I'll have to muster up the deepest wells of my super-
> hero dexterity to get out of

Or not.

See: there's a girl lying next to me
in my bed,
In the dark,
Here in my dorm room.
She's naked. We've just had sex.
I guess you can call her my girlfriend
Cause yes,
She's naked
She's lying next to me
And we've just had sex?

This is a new thing for me, this girl
so you'll understand my hesitation —
First time, you know, doing the ol'
in out in out
and stuff.

Yeah, we've been through those cagey first conversations
where you talk over each others sentences
But we haven't crossed that threshold,
where suddenly it's like
This one might be around for a spell, she's shared such and such
I've shared such and such
We're not talking over each other's sentences anymore

All the stuff that adds up to
Intimacy.

Nope. We haven't gotten there yet.
Nope. We're in the middle of the post-first-time-humping awk-
ward silence.
And let me emphasize that this post-first-time silence is incred-
ibly meaningful —
The whole future of the relationship hovers over that silence
Like a promise
Like a threat.

DARK PLAY; OR STORIES FOR BOYS
Carlos Murillo

Dramatic
Nick, late teens, early twenties

> *Adam is another boy whose life Nick has destroyed by pretending to be someone else on the Internet. Here he describes the exhilaration he feels about what he has done.*

NICK: I remember lying on the pavement
>> Feeling a smile spread across my face
>> The silhouette of Adam against the blue southern California sky
>> hovering above me for a second before he ran . . .

> That's when I felt it
> A wave
> A hurricane
> An earthquake
> Mt. St. Helen's blowing her top.
> A cloudburst and
> A shower of wine
> A swirl of color
> Disappearing outlines
> The sky splitting open
> Levitating me
> A gazillion tiny lightbulbs
> Twinkling through the pores of my skin
> The Virgin Mary and Mary Magdalene
> Caressing,
> Kissing
> licking
> my skin
> a skyscraper collapsing

a mother giving birth
No ME
I love you
No ME
I love you
Fire
Water

Light
Air
White.
I love you.

If this is what death is like.

I want to die every day.

But I lived.

THE DARLINGS
Susan Eve Haar

Comic
George, forty-two

> *George is a CEO and a white-collar criminal. His wife, who he has been trying to tell that he is about to be indicted, has just left to accept an award from the Junior League for her work with "brownish children." Here he is addressing his dog, Nana.*

GEORGE: Skol. They want to make an example of me. Flush me out of the system like some kind of sewage — Well, believe me, I'm not going down easy. Screw them all. Who do they think they're dealing with? I mean, hey, I employ eighteen hundred people. Is that sanctimonious son of a bitch thinking about them? No way. All he's thinking about is re-election. I mean, sure, I did some stuff. You got to push the envelope a little, that's how you make it happen! There's nothing I did that anybody else in my position wouldn't do! *(Takes a gulp.)* The money, the money. That's all they wanna talk about. They just don't get it — money's what happens when you're making art. *(Sings to Nana.)* All my hopes and schemes! All my hopes and schemes! See, you steal because — But I didn't steal! I simply took advantage of an opportunity that was uniquely mine! And those prosecutors, those pissants, they just don't understand. Those lackies, with their badges and their forty-three thou a year, they don't know what it takes to be a master of the universe. I turned around more companies than you chewed up slippers. And when I sold, and how I sold, hey, I got friends. I play golf. I play squash. You hear things. You got instincts. You'd think they'd have something better to do. The world is not a safe place and what are they doing? They got teams of accountants, working like termites, going through my stuff. Everything. Jesus. God, you've heard it all. My one true friend. If you could talk, I'd have to put you in the shredder. Hey, just kidding. Have another. *(He kisses Nana affectionately.)* There would be no love in this house if it wasn't for you. So where is the love of my life? *(Looks at watch.)* Out with the orphans. And she didn't even ask me what I did. Unbelievable. Hey, I could be an ax murderer as long as the Visa bill gets paid. *(Swigs.)* But you know — she still gets to me. She's under my skin, like ringworm. It's amazing. After all this time, I just want to tie her up with her Gucci scarves and bang the hell out of her. But maybe wanting her's just another bad habit, you tell me. Not talking? You're one smart puppy. *(He kisses Nana.)* Hey, I know she's tough to live with. But, God, she can be so tender — When I first met her, she was this radiant girl, I was afraid to touch her. And she knew things. Like . . . how to eat an artichoke. Special. She made me feel special. Everything I wanted in one package and I thought we'd make beautiful babies together, and nothing else mattered. What happened? The girl who was my sweetheart, she's long gone. I mean she she's still here, but where's the girl I fell in love with? The girl with the elusive smile? She's shopping.

DEDICATION; OR, THE STUFF OF DREAMS

Terrence McNally

Comic
Lou, forties

> *Lou runs a small children's theater company. Here he has gotten
> started about a playwright for whom he has a particular dislike —
> William Shakespeare.*

LOU: I hate Shakespeare. I don't know anyone who's honest who doesn't.
In the first place, there's too many words. He said so himself: "Words,
words, words." And what are they talking about? "Speak English," I
want to yell at the actors. No, instead you get yada yada yada in iambic
pentameter for six and a half hours. And the plots! People getting mur-
dered because they lost a handkerchief. Women playing men and no
one notices. "What's with the high voice, buddy? And what are those,
pray tell, oh shepherd youth? Look like hooters to me." The plays
are so confusing people don't even know what period to set them in.
The Scottish Play on the North Pole in 3005 — I'm sorry, I'm very
confused. I don't deny Shakespeare wrote a lot of great lines. "To be
or not to be." "Et tu, Brute?" "Let's kill all the lawyers." It's just the
goddamn plays you have to sit through to get to them! King Lear or
Dumbo, there's no contest.

DEDICATION; OR, THE STUFF OF DREAMS

Terrence McNally

Seriocomic
Lou, forties

> *Lou runs a small children's theater company. He has the opportunity to move his company to a ratty old ex-vaudeville house. His techie has gone down into a trap to check what's below the stage, leaving Lou alone to ruminate on his life in children's theater.*

LOU: So, here I am, center stage, solus, on a real stage in a real theater. A stage and theater that by rights should belong to me and not some alcoholic millionaire who is letting it go beyond all repair or reason. By what rights is it mine? Divine rights, artistic rights, moral ones. Not that they count for much in these impoverished times when wealth equals good and big equals better. I would transform this shabby, forgotten, forlorn room into a place of wonder and imagination again. That chandelier would sparkle anew if I had to polish every crystal myself. The aisles would be newly carpeted in a gesture of welcome and respect. Those rows of broken seats would be reclaimed in a plush red velvet that said, "Sit down, children, you are safe here. We are going to take you on a wonderful journey to China or Persia or Timbuktu." Today we are going to tell you the amazing story of your favorite character, anyone you choose. But before we begin, there are a few rules, so listen up. I said listen up, you kids in the balcony. That means you, too. No kicking the seat in front of you. No paper airplanes or spitballs. No putting chewing gum under the arms or seat of your chair. No talking, unless the action becomes so unbearably exciting that you have to call out: "Turn around, Robin Hood, quick, the Sheriff is going to kill you." Or so sad that you won't be able to live if you don't speak up. It's up to you that Tinker Bell doesn't die, that Abraham doesn't sacrifice his firstborn. For the precious time that you are here and we actors are before you, the future of the world is in your hands, the fate of the human race is yours to decide. Think about it. The possibilities are boundless, the responsibility is yours. And don't forget to breathe! I know, we all forget sometimes in the theater. Me, too. I also stop breathing, it's so wonderful. *(He takes a deep breath, then lets it out.)* And always the curtain will fall, the story will have ended, and we actors will take our bows. Houselights up! It's over. We can all go home now. But something has changed. Tinker Bell has lived. Cinderella has found her Prince. You will go back to your real world and it will still be raw and painful, ugly even, but maybe a little less so because of what you have seen here today. Harmony and happiness were possible. And I will go back to my real world and it, too, will be a little more bearable, a little less unbearable because of what I have given you — and in giving you, have given myself: love and laughter, which are a good deal more nourishing at your age than bread and games. Hell, at any age. You lucky, lucky children. When I was your age, I didn't have a theater in my life. I had to invent one of my own. All I had was a mirror, my mother's closet, and my music. *(Strains of Tchaikovsky's* Sleeping Beauty.*)* I'm telling you a secret now. A secret no one knows but you — not even Jessie, and I tell her everything. Well, almost everything. I would go to my mother's closet and take out her fullest skirt. I would put on the music I loved the best, the *Sleeping Beauty* — it was a waltz — and start to twirl in front of the mirror. Slow, slow I'd twirl, in-a-trance-kind-of slow. For hours sometimes. It felt like forever.

DIRECT FROM DEATH ROW
THE SCOTTSBORO BOYS
Mark Stein

Dramatic
Knight, fifties to sixties

> *Here Knight, the state Attorney General, is asking one and all why*
> *the Scottsboro Boys were put on trial for the rape and murder of two*
> *white girls.*

KNIGHT: Yeah, well, problem was, there came to be a good deal more to
this case than evidence. For one thing, we had ol' Joe and his Commie pals holdin' rallies all over the world! Issuin' demands on Alabama!
Now if we'd allowed that tactic to succeed, think what would be next.
Plus, we had the likes of Sam here steppin' off the train. Now I take
pride in Southern hospitality. But Sam's arrival was just a bit too rem-
iniscent of the days of Reconstruction, when carpetbaggers came down
here, claimin' to possess a superior morality, and tellin' us how to go
about our affairs. Say, let's sing one of the great songs from Reconstruction! Gimme an intro, Skip. *(The piano player thinks, then shrugs.)*
Guess there *aren't* any great songs from Reconstruction. Wonder why
that is. Here's what it all boils down to. We've never come to grips
with five words a few of our Foundin' Fathers sort of slipped in on
us. "All men are created equal." I, for one, have never found where
in the Bible the Creator says that — but be that as it may. If it *is* the
case, then the colored race will build their community to a level equal
to that of the whites. And if they are not equal, quite frankly, they
will remain somethin' less. Or maybe become somethin' *more* I sup-
pose I should add! Or maybe just become somethin' different. Which
is all right. For that is our coat of many colors. Why did we persist
in the prosecution of these boys? Not just to preserve Southern cul-
ture, but *all* our cultures. Which is to say, America.

DIRECT FROM DEATH ROW
THE SCOTTSBORO BOYS
Mark Stein

Dramatic

Haywood, black, eighteen when he was arrested, but he could be any age
  now

*Haywood is one of the Scottsboro Boys, who were tried and convicted
of the rape and murder of two white girls.*

HAYWOOD: *(Shaken, ashamed.)* Well . . . the beans is spilled now, I guess.
Needless to say, so much for the pardon. *(Takes a moment to collect
himself, but, upset, he isn't getting collected.)* How 'bout it, Eugene?
Maybe sing one o' your faggot songs, why don't ya? Oughta be real
touchin'. *(No answer. Eugene turns away. Pulling himself together to some
degree.)* After that episode, Alabama say the case is closed. They say
from here on out . . . *(Finding his voice wavering here:)* . . . there be
no more Scottsboro Boys. *(A breath.)* We handle their cases one at a
time. Five years later, they let Charlie out real quiet. And a little after
that, I shakes hands with my old friend Andy, and shake Clarence's
hand, too. Even Ozie, despite stabbin' the sheriff, go free in, I dunno,
1946 or somethin'. Only one left after that is me. Way I see it, everyone I ever known has let me down. Or else, like my mama, has died
and gone. Liebowitz and all them do-gooders let me down. God
knows the governor let me down. And God Himself, I sometimes feel,
let me down, too. Only one left to depend on now is me. So I fixes
on a plan. They got me sweepin' floors inside the prison. But where
I needs to be is out on the farm. So I get myself in a little trouble
and they bring me to the warden for a whippin'. And I make just like
Brer Rabbit. "Oh don't send me to the farm, cap'n! Whip me if you
gotta but please don't be sendin' me to the farm!" Which o' course
they do. But I'm assigned to Shotgun Smith, and ain't nobody ever
escaped from him. Though there be several that died tryin'. All I can
do is . . . be patient. Then in the winter of '48, he retire. And they

put a rookie in his place. But still I bide my time. 'Til well into summer, when the leaves be full and the corn be high. And I invited several others to go with me, pointin' out how good their chances is, on accounta the guards first be sendin' the hounds after me. But really what I be usin' 'em for was bait. Come mid-July, I decide the time has come to grant myself a pardon. So as the sun be startin' to set one day, I give the nod, and we scatter through the corn! One young kid I kept with me, case I needed a sacrifice. The others head out as fast and far as possible, the fools. Me and the boy, we stay close, listenin' to the dogs gradually roundin' all them others up. After dark, me and the boy ease into the woods. But then he start talkin' about stealin' a car to get away. I tell him forget that. But them dogs barkin' is makin' him scared. Across the road there be a farm and he decide to make a dash for their garage. No sooner he start off runnin' than there's shouts and shots. Shit, I'm thinkin', that gonna draw the dogs for sure! I don't know what become of that boy, but me I double back to where there be a stream about waist-high. Figure maybe the water hide my scent. But damn if them dogs ain't comin' closer. And through the trees, I see the headlights pullin' up on the road. A whole posse of 'em. The dogs I can tell is comin' through the cornfield. Next they be here in the woods. Ain't nothin' for it now, Haywood — 'lessn you can make yourself into a snake. Them dogs already splashin' in the water. I can see 'em. Two that's jumped on in and one be waitin' at the edge, woofin' and wailin'. Good boy. You a good boy. That lead dog he look at me sorta funny, still goin' arf! arf! arf! Come here, boy. People be treatin' you like a dog all your life, c'mere to me. Come on. And the second dog too now start watchin' kinda close. Yeah, you a good boy. C'mere to Haywood. And that front dog kind of nuzzle on up to me, and I take his head in my hands and thrust it under the water. And to the second one I be sayin', "Oh, he's a good dog. And you a good dog too, you know that?" And underwater I feel that hound kickin' and strugglin'. "C'mon to me, boy," I say to that second dog, who be lookin' at me kinda queer now. "Come on over here to Haywood." And the first dog, he finally beginnin' to slow down under the water there. And when he stop, I reach out to the second one and say, "It's OK. Come to Haywood." And I kill him too, same as the first. And that dog over by the edge, he ain't sayin' nothin'. He don't seem to know what all's goin' on. C'mere boy. You a good dog, too. But I don't guess he believed that, since he just turned and hunkered off. All the next day I stay on the prison grounds, knowin' it be the last place they look. And then I set out, travelling at night through the stream . . . like a snake.

DISCONNECT
Rob Ackerman

Dramatic
Steve, late thirties

> *Steve, a marketing consultant, has invited a couple, who are near strangers, to dinner at his home. Here, he tells his guests and his wife what he realized while at a marketing conference from which he has just returned.*

STEVE: There's a problem. Pete calls it a "Perception Problem." That's good, Pete. I like that. People perceive something, sense that something's not right. And it's everywhere, this problem, up and down the charts. It happens once a month when they write their checks or click on Quicken or do whatever they do to figure out how costly their lives have become, wondering why they've got thirty-six fifty in taxes and surcharges on a seventy dollar statement and "portability fees" and "network access fees" and "excise fees," and . . . *(Abruptly.)* OK fine, done. Spend forty million on commercials with grandpa on the phone on the sun porch and sixty million on spots with sports stars sending text message to babes in belly shirts, and pretty soon everybody's gonna feel like they absolutely have to have a cell phone, but the question is — do they? *(Again shifting quickly.)* I know, I know, "We make it and market it, we don't moralize about it." But why can't we stop to think? Doesn't anything matter to us? Within our lifetimes, objects of value pass from elegant to useful to neglected to obsolete to memory. Let me just ask you something: Why is the woman on our billboards pulling an alphanumeric pager from her purse? Is she showing us a better way to live? Or is she just finding a new way to talk too much? We just say what we need to say to sell the most stuff — not the best stuff, not the most helpful stuff, just the most stuff — and I know it's not the American Way, but if we give up a little profit now we could gain a lot of loyalty later, start building back people's trust. We'd still be greedy, just not so egregiously greedy. But greed is still good. What do you say, Pete? It could work.

DISCONNECT
Rob Ackerman

Dramatic
Steve, late thirties

> *Steve, a marketing consultant, has invited a couple, who are near*
> *strangers, to dinner at his home. While the wives are out of the room,*
> *he tells his guest Fred about a sexual encounter arranged for him at*
> *a recent marketing conference by a colleague, and what he learned*
> *from it.*

STEVE: So I get this call from this guy Pete Hamish and he's all somber
and severe which is part of his whole alpha male act, you know. He's
the lion who growls the loudest and suns himself on the highest rock.
And he calls to wish me a happy birthday and I'm wondering how
he even knows it's my birthday and all of a sudden this *woman* shows
up in my office, this unbelievable woman. She's wearing a tasteful
floor-length coat and she smells like orange blossoms in Seville. She
smells good is how she smells. And she's also staggeringly beautiful,
almost beyond what you would believe is possible, like a total sexual
fantasy: long dark hair and smooth olive skin. These are obviously
not inexpensive services the guy has purchased here. And she's unbuttoning her coat and she's looking at me as she's unbuttoning. She's
got like a laser lock-down on my eyes. All these people around me
are laughing and shouting, but she's completely serious. This seems
to really mean something to her. And when her coat falls to the floor,
it turns out she's wearing very little, just this little satin whatever. And
next thing I know I'm feeling her weight, not a lot of weight, just
kind of the ideal amount, and also her hair and her skin and that
humid slippery satin on . . . on ME.

   . . . OK, so the satin thing that she's wearing up top, it has a
clasp in front, and she's hovering above me on my Herman Miller
office chair and she reaches down and takes my hand and lifts it to
this clasp, and suddenly her breasts are there and they're powdered

and perfect and I mean, "I'm gonna die here" is what I'm thinking. And of course there's a big laugh and all this locker room stuff, but it's like I'm in a glass tunnel with this woman, this green-eyed woman, and . . .

. . . OK. Finally, I broke eye contact. I mean, I had to.

. . . Just to, you know, take a look.

. . . And what I saw were . . .

. . . Incisions.

. . . Scars. I mean scars. They were almost invisible but for some reason they were all I could see. I mean I am looking at these supposedly perfect tits and all I see are these scars. All I can think is that she's fake. This is fake. It's all fake. And when I look to her eyes again it's like it's over. It has ended. She knows and I know, so she leans down and kisses me on the cheek and she's gone.

DRACULA RIDES AGAIN
Jeff Goode

Comic
Doc, thirties to forties

This is a Wild West comedy that brings together various monster-movie archetypes. Here, Doc Frankenstein tells the townsfolk who and what the mysterious stranger who's know as the Count is, and why he has come to their town.

DOC: What Miss Della is trying to say, as delicately as she can, is that the Count is missing today, not because he's afraid of me. But because he's afraid of getting a tan!

. . . *(Jovially:)* I shouldn't toy with Miss Della like this. You see, the truth of the matter is that Miss Della and I are both tellin' you a pack of lies, and I think we could both go on tossin' buffalo chips until the cows come home and it won't get us any closer to the truth.

. . . The truth is — and I think Miss Della will back me up on this — that the Count is neither yellow-bellied, nor a coward. And in eight or nine hours, when the sun goes down, I imagine he'll show up here and prove it by shootin' me down like a dog in the street. And then he's gonna shoot anyone else who called him a coward just now.

. . . And there won't be nothing any of us can do about it. Because in reality, the Count is not afraid of me or you or any man living. Or woman either, for that matter. And he's missing today not because he has sensitive eyes, or a skin condition, or a dentist's appointment that's keeping him from facin' me right now. No, the Count won't meet me today or any day, because he's a creature of the night. A vampire. A blood-sucking monster straight out of hell. And the truth is, he didn't come to Tombstone to set you free! HE CAME TO SUCK YOUR BLOOD!

. . . And there is something else you should know about your brave hero. You all know him as "The Count," but his real name is Dracula. Count Dracula.

. . . And like all Europeans, he wants . . . only one thing from you.

. . . HE WANTS TO SUCK YOUR BLOOD!

THE FIRST ANNUAL ACHADAMEE AWARDS
Alan Haehnel

Comic
Nigel, teens

Nigel is before his class, presenting a paper he has written.

NIGEL: Before I begin my oral presentation on the play *Hamlet*, I would like to take just a moment to clear the air about a few things. I understand that some nasty rumors have been going around about me. Rumor one: I have never even read the play *Hamlet*. The book has been in the bottom of my locker, unopened since the first day we got the assignment. Rumor two: I don't know a thing about *Hamlet*. Up until yesterday morning, I thought a *Hamlet* was a clever name for a small breakfast item. According to that rumor, I even went to Denny's and tried to order a Hamlet with a side of home fries. Rumor three: I am completely unprepared for this presentation, and all I plan to do is get a barely passing grade by standing up here and bluffing my way through until my time is up. And rumor four, the most sickening one of all: I, Nigel Thorburn, have no academic motivation whatsoever. I expend the least amount of energy possible to squeak by, using only my natural charm and extreme talents in the art of slinging the bull. I want to say, right here and right now, that I highly resent these rumors. If any of you have been spreading them, I say — pardon my language, please — damn you. Damn your conniving hearts and your lying mouths. To those of you who have begun to doubt me because of these rumors, I say listen! For I am about to deliver a presentation on *Hamlet* that will erase all doubt, all fear, all worry, all . . . excuse me? What? My time is up? Do you mean to say I'll be getting a D- for simply using up my time even though I haven't yet begun to reveal the great mysteries of the play *Hamlet?* I will? I am appalled. But, I accept my fate without complaint. Hey, that almost rhymed. I am good!

HOME FRONT
Greg Owens

Dramatic
Ronnie, seventeen

> *Ronnie is speaking to a woman whose head is bandaged and whom*
> *he assumes to be an American soldier named Lucy who has been mis-*
> *takenly placed with Ronnie's parents by Commander Abraham Lin-*
> *coln of Central Security after a secret military experiment that went*
> *wrong.*

RONNIE: So you were in the shit, huh? Cool. D'you see a lot of action? I
mean before you . . . *(Pause.)* I'm thinking about enlisting myself. If
I don't get a baseball scholarship. I'd wanna be on the front lines. Get
in the real shit, y'know? Can't you talk? I don't know if you can even
understand a word I'm saying. My dad was a fighter pilot in Viet-
nam. Flew over two hundred missions. He bombed the crap outta
those Commie gooks. They gave him a medal too. I'd show it to ya,
but I don't know for sure where he keeps it. *(Pause.)* Dad always says
that going to war is the most intense experience he thinks a human
being can have. It pushes you to all your limits. Body, mind, and soul.
Is that how you felt? I'm intense. I don't think war's anything I
couldn't handle. I thrive on pressure. And I'm at my best under challenging conditions. That's why I didn't mind giving up my room to
you. Sleeping on the couch is nothing. I spent a month at a wilder-
ness camp in Idaho one time, y'know? Well, actually it wasn't a camp.
It was more of a . . . program. One of those places they send you when
you get in trouble so you can learn discipline and teamwork and self-
control and all that shit. *(Beat.)* I had to go there after I kicked the
shit out of this kid at school. He didn't really do anything to me. So
it was kinda wrong. I just did it really for fun. He was a total fag.
So he sorta had it coming. I guess I shouldn't have done it though.
That kind of thing looks bad on your record when you're applying
for college. At this camp they taught us how to dig latrines and set

signal fires and make snares to catch rabbits and hunt berries and roots and shit. We learned a lot of cool shit. It was pretty tough. We also had to do a lot of hiking. With forty pounds of gear on our backs. *(Beat.)* I think I could handle war. Don't you?

HOW HIS BRIDE CAME TO ABRAHAM
Karen Sunde

Dramatic
Abe, teens to twenties

> *Abe is an Israeli soldier. By nature he is tender and bright, but he has been coarsened by grueling duty. He has been wounded by a roadside bomb and has taken shelter with a mysterious captive who is tending his wound. This is his answer when she asks, "How many Arabs have you killed?"*

ABE: Sabra, listen. I asked for this. I transferred here, out of Israel, so I wouldn't wind up killing children! I don't like this. You think I want to kill someone? I don't hate Arabs. I only want to live in peace. But they keep on coming to kill us.

   And I'll tell you, it's not like you think. They've got no chance here. No chance to win. To even fight. I've seen it work. One night on ambush, I crawled back to the A P C, the tank, and inside, they're watching with a night-scope, on a screen, like a video cartoon! And there come the stick creatures. They show up on the screen because they're alive out there, they're warm, they're moving — not even close, a whole kilometer away! And because it's night, we don't ask — we just fire. We fire, several rounds, and every shell seeks warmth, and bursts itself in flesh. We watch. In silence . . . the creatures falter on the screen. No shrieks. Nothing. The stick shapes just begin to fade, getting dimmer as their warmth is lost, until they blank out, blending with the screen, completely cold. *(Pause.)* No. I've never *seen* anyone die.

   . . . *(Shouts.)* I'm protecting the border, farmers two kilometers from here! Am I allowed to defend my home?!

THE IMAGINARY INVALID
Molière
Translated/adapted by James Magruder

Comic
Diafoirus, fifties to sixties

> *This new version of Molière's classic has a very contemporary feel to
> it. Diafoirus is a quack doctor, here extolling the virtues of his dim
> son to his best patient, a hypochondriac named Argan.*

DIAFOIRUS: I don't just say this because I'm his father, but I have every right
to be proud of him. Anyone who has ever met him tells me he is a
boy completely free of guile and malice. His imagination has never
been keen, and he hasn't the sparkling wit of other young men, but
that's exactly the reason why I predicted a great future for him in med-
icine. As a child, he was never what you would call lively or alert. He
was phlegmatic, practically mute, and utterly uninterested in child-
ish games. Why, a simple piece of string could occupy him for days.
And oh what a time we had teaching him to read! He was nine years
old before he learned the alphabet. "Well," I said to myself, "the tardy
trees bear the best fruit. It may be harder to write on marble than on
sand, but things last longer when you do, so his slow comprehension
and his dull imagination are but the harbingers of a sound judgment
to come." I won't say that college was easy for him, but he steeled
himself against all difficulties, and his professors always gave him high
marks for industry. Finally, through sheer hard work, perseverance and
flash cards, he received his diploma. And I can say without a trace of
vanity that during the two years since he took his bachelor's degree,
there hasn't been another candidate who has aroused such attention
and critical commentary from our faculty. His reputation is formi-
dable, and a proposition hasn't yet been put forth among us that he
hasn't advocated to the death the contrary position. He's steadfast in
a dispute, strong as a Turk in his principles, never retracts an opin-
ion, and pursues his argument to the furthest limits of logic. But what

delights me most of all about him, and in which he follows my professional example, is his blind, unswerving adherence to the opinions of the ancients. He refuses to comprehend, or even entertain, the research and reasoning behind these so-called medical discoveries of our century, like the circulation of the blood and other crack-witted twaddle.

IN A KINGDOM BY THE SEA

Karen Sunde

Dramatic
Hogan, forties

> *Hogan is a colonel in the U.S. Marines. He is a hearty, wise-cracking, larger-than-life character. He has just been abducted by Muslim terrorists. In this direct address to the audience he tells us about how the key to understanding America is football.*

HOGAN: *(To audience.)* You want the key to America? One word? *Football.* So I'd say to Laurel, *(Dramatic.)* "I can see them coming . . . right up the field, barreling, every single one over 300 pounds. They'll crush me, punc-tuate my sweet body with their brutal cleats. I'm gonna hurt sooo much. They're gonna kill me tonight!"

Then she'd hang onto the locker, double over laughing — "Hogie, you un-regenerate, un-mitigated dumbhead! Why do you do it?! Don't go out for the team. Be the *mascot.* You could waddle out there just the same." *(Picks up football.)* What could I say to her?

Should I have asked her what she sees? Jumping up, shrieking . . . her dimpled knees red as cheeks? What's she see that's so god-damned exciting in some muddy heap sprawled and grunting on the ten-yard line? If she can answer me that, then I'll know why I do it.

(Hogan feints a throw, turns abruptly.)

But life is like that. Everything gets you ready. And it's not only the girls. It's the moms, the dads, the *alums* for God's sake, and the coach, the whole bald-assed town! They're all on their feet. It's like you're them, and they want you in the goddamned pile — ramming, crunching, dropping those 300 pounders dead!

All you can hope is that somehow you'll get onto the field with all those pads and that gigantic helmet . . . that you won't stumble halfway out and go flat on your face without ever making it to the goddamned pile. Does a woman think of that? The only time I could figure why anyone would do it — and I *told* Laurel — was when you'd get free of the pile . . .

(Hogan rises, weaving the ball slowly back and forth.)

. . . I mean really break out, and it was just you, just you, dodging the snags, leaping past all those lunging hulks, finally you, taking off, running wild, soaring down the field, carried on the screaming wave of climax in everyone's throat and chest and thighs. *(Beat.)* And that's America!

(Hogan tosses the ball high, turns to retrieve his Marine hat . . . The ball is gone.)

IN A KINGDOM BY THE SEA

Karen Sunde

Dramatic
Hogan, forties

> *Hogan is a colonel in the U.S. Marines. He is a hearty, wise-cracking, larger-than-life character. He tells us about a recent truck-bomb attack by Muslim terrorists.*

HOGAN: No Marine ever, *ever* fired without being fired upon! We went there in good faith; and they threw roses. Roses! We had strict rules — we could not fire. And by God we upheld them! *(Shaken.)* and American boys believed, *believed*, that some good was being served. At home they said no one was being shot at; the dying boys were only accidents. Until . . . the barracks blew up.

> *(Seeing the past, Hogan relives the explosion, begins calm, still:)*

Sunrise over Beirut, golden wash, gleaming, pastels . . . astonishing. And Sunday. The boys are nested, having a last dream, an extra half hour. *(Beat.)* I saw the grin. Like he was sharing a secret. Dark beard, dark blue shirt, blurred past the gate. His big truck, yellow, sitting alone in the lobby, looked silly. Then came the orange white flash, too loud to hear, glued skin to my cheekbones, wind . . . lifted the rooms, pulled out their air, set four stories down in one pile.

Some boys woke with their ceiling in bed, and the floor above and its ceiling and the next, too strange to believe. They said God, oh God help me. Now I lay be down to sleep. The boys covered in ash, scattered, parts without arms, without heads, caught in trees, never woke, but were found by boys who never slept after. And the boys with head and arm hanging free, bodies crushed between slabs, dripping slow . . . red on grey ash, when they woke, those were the worst.

> *(Hogan stands still, unable to speak.)*

IN A KINGDOM BY THE SEA

Karen Sunde

Dramatic
Hogan, forties

> *Hogan is a colonel in the U.S. Marines. He is a hearty, wise-cracking, larger-than-life character. Sami, his unit's Information Officer, has accused him of coming to Lebanon for "payback."*

HOGAN: Most of you don't remember, but there was a time in America when uniform equaled hero. Boys got their manhood in one quick change. Girls shivered with the pleasure of exclusion. Back in the sweet sweet 50s, with everything just getting better and better, and more and more, but then . . . well, the uniform took a dive, you might say.

But let's get one thing straight. The trouble was not the dream. The American dream was about money. And that'll always be sweet. No. The trouble was the "Ideal." I mean, whoever heard of a country based on the "Principle" that all men are created etc., etc. And on top of that comes the idiotic idea that we're good or *honest?!* Right away we should have known we were in the shit. I mean, a country *is* because your people belong, not because you "believe" in it.

But what the hell. We had youth, we had money . . . Except, hold it: What happens when your whole identity is riding on this "ideal" of being good, and it takes you to 'Nam? Gives you the finger? Involves every damn soldier in genocide?

Well I say, you crack. Who could survive? You crack. And so we did. The uniform was tarnished. The girls didn't catch their breath anymore. But when in doubt, stand stronger. That's what I figured. Believe twice as hard. So I stood. And I *believed.*

And I wound up here.

LARRY AND THE WEREWOLF
Jeff Goode

Comic
Second Centurion, could be any age

> *The Second Centurion, a proud Roman warrior, realizes that he is a mere spear-carrier upon the stage of someone else's life, which is driving him nuts.*

SECOND CENTURION: *(Shrieking out of control:)* WHO THE HELL IS CHRIST?!??!?! Great Jupiter, we're a flashback! We're living in a flashback! None of this is really happening. We're just reliving the past so someone in the future can go on with their story. But what about us? What about me? Don't I have a story? Do I make general? Command a Roman legion? What about my family? My children? Do I have children? Where am I now? Am I famous? Or am I already dead? Rotting in some Tunisian desert or sunk in a galley at the bottom of the Nile? *(To the audience:)* What happens to me? Somebody please tell me! *(Beat.)* They just sit there. They don't know! They don't know me. Maybe I'm not even a main character. Maybe I'm just the Second Centurion — part of the human backdrop against which the real characters play their hour upon life's stage. After this scene I don't even exist! Is that it? Oh, please, God, don't let me be a flashback. I WANT A LIFE, TOO! I have hopes, dreams, aspirations. I'm complex! I'm fascinating! Oh, God! Oh, God! I'm going into post-traumatic shock! *(He goes into post-traumatic shock.)*

LARRY AND THE WEREWOLF
Jeff Goode

Comic
Dick Piston, thirties to forties

> *Dick Piston, an incompetent hotel detective who aspires to be a hard-boiled film-noir dick, recalls the incomprehensible twists and turns in his latest botched case.*

PISTON: Death has a way of clearing things up. My sinuses for one. And priorities. I knew now that solving this case was more than just a hobby. More than a job. More than an adventure. . . . Whatever that would be. Call it love. Call it Ishmael, but I knew that at the end of this proverbial rainbow was a pot of gold that could suck the chrome off a set of hubcaps. One kiss told me that. And all I had to do was catch a killer.

    . . . Herberto Hermosa was dead. Murdered. Snatched from the tender clutches of holy matrimony and torn into a half dozen bloody bite-size morsels. Why? Because that's what werewolves do. Wolfgang Biedermann was dead, too. Murdered by me when I discovered that he *was* that werewolf. Or so I thought. And Columbus thought he discovered India, but it don't make New York New Delhi. Y'see, lead bullets won't kill a werewolf. But that's what I pumped Biedermann full of after somebody removed the silver bullets from my gun. So Biedermann is an innocent man . . . Was an innocent man. . . . No, he's *still* an innocent man. Just a dead one, that's all. Then there's me. Dick Piston, hotel detective. Trapped on the tenth floor of said hotel as it burned to the ground, I leaped to my death only to survive only to die at the hands of whoever's hands they were that were sent to murder me in my hospital bed. Cruel hands. Somewhat sticky hands. Hired hands in the employ of Cabal the hotel manager. Why? Because I was getting too close. Because Cabal didn't want me finding out what she already knew — that the werewolf who murdered Herberto Hermosa at the Lakeview Hotel still works at the Lakeview

41

Hotel. Because Cabal the hotel manager *is* the werewolf! *(Then he notices Cabal's body.)* Damn. *(Pause.)* Whoever stole the silver bullets from my gun must have known Cabal was a werewolf and used those bullets to . . . *(He looks at Cabal again.)* Wait, you were bludgeoned. *(Pause.)* Dammit, I've wasted another ten minutes and I'm no closer to the solution than when I was dead.

LA TEMPESTAD
Larry Loebell

Comic
Alonso, fifties

This play is an updating of Shakespeare's The Tempest *set in the present. Alonso is a military man, here telling Ariel that he better tell his boss, Prospero, that the time is now to get serious about the terrorist threat.*

ALONSO: He wants to see me? He thinks he can command and I will come running? Who the fuck does he think he is?

. . . I have plenty on my plate at this particular moment. Do you think I don't know he's pissed off? Do you think I don't know he's going to do everything he can to drive a truckload of bad press and blame up my ass?

. . . This isn't some little pissant operation we got here. I have a dead pilot who's got parents, too, and they aren't coming down here to parade their grief in front of the wire service photographers and point fingers of blame. They're waiting for the body at Dover where there will be no pictures of their bravery. They attend their grief in private like . . .

. . . I have half of the Fourth Fleet sitting out there waiting to get back to work. You think we're going to stop because one of our planes went down?

. . . You tell your boss that terrorism creeps in when you let your guard down.

. . . That's the lesson of our time. You respond with passivity, the next thing that happens is boatloads of radicalized fanatics are landing on your beaches with dirty bombs in their Zodiacs. You think Bin Laden gives a crap about the fine distinction between this island and that, or mainland versus Caribbean? You're safe because this base is here. America is safer because of what we are doing here. And the more of these guys we learn to dig out of their hidey holes, the safer we'll all be.

. . . So here's the deal. You tell your Mister Prospero, when we start our training runs again, he should watch from his veranda. Tell him to get that Caliban fellow to mix him up a double rum planter's punch. Then you tell him to turn his eyes to the sky. You watch with him, too. And you will see the glory of U.S. air power coming in, as it has done for the last sixty years and as it will for the next sixty, and then you thank your lucky stars that you live in this country and not in one of those places that would as soon cut your throat as look at you.

. . . You tell him. Freedom costs.

LOOKING
Norm Foster

Dramatic
Matt, forties to early fifties

> Looking *is a comedy set in a tennis club about people looking for love. Here Matt is declaring his love for Nina.*

MATT: I've got something to say to you, Nina. Now, I tried saying it the other night and you told me I made you sick but I'm going to give it another shot anyway because I just don't know when to quit. I'm like Andy here. Like some idiot who's willing to keep trying even though it's futile. Even though his heart is going to get stomped into the ground. Even though . . .

. . . And who knows, maybe I didn't say it right the first time. Maybe my inflection was all wrong. Although I am a broadcaster by trade and it is my job to communicate so I doubt if that was it. Maybe you just weren't listening. Maybe in your haste to get rid of me and wallow in self-doubt, you didn't hear what I said. So here it is again. And listen closely because I'm only going to say this twenty or thirty more times. Nina, I'm crazy about you. I am. And I'm telling you right here in front of everybody in this bar. I don't care who hears it!

. . . I don't care! Did you hear me that time, Nina? I'm crazy about you. And I don't want this to end before we've given it a real solid try. And if you still want some time, then that's fine. If you want to go slow, we'll go as slow as you want, I'm in no rush because I happen to think you're worth the wait, so I'll wait. I'll wait as long as it takes. Because I think we're good together. No, hell, I think we're great together. And I can't live without you. All right, that's a bit much. Of course I could live without you. What am I gonna do? Die? No. I'll go on living, meet somebody else, settle down with her, and that'll be that. But I would much rather be with you than her! So that's it. That's what I wanted to say. I'm crazy about you Nina, and if you don't give me a chance to be the love of your life then the rest of my life will seem like a drive down a dark and endless road.

. . . *(To Val.)* And you! What's your problem? This is a sweet guy. give him a chance for God's sake! What the hell is wrong with you women!? *(To Nina.)* So, what do you say, Nina? Do I still make you sick, or do you want to smarten the hell up and give this thing a try? Or do you want me to tell you again? Huh? Because I will if you force me to.

LOOKING
Norm Foster

Seriocomic
Andy, forties to fifties

> Looking *is a comedy set in a tennis club about looking for love. Here*
> *Andy, something of a perpetual failure, pleads his case with the*
> *woman he loves, Val.*

ANDY: Well, there's no need to lie to try and impress you now, right? I mean, there's nothing happening here, so I can just be myself like you said.

. . . There's not much to me, so I have to lie to bring myself up to your level.

. . . Yeah. I mean, a woman like you? What would you want with a guy like me? Hell, I can't even keep a business running. And it's not like it was a challenge, right? Selling storage space? How hard can that be? Too hard for me apparently. I've got a new job though. Yeah. I'm a security guard. I start Monday. I'll be trying to stop demented jazz fans from rushing the studio and lighting mood candles. Yeah, I'm pretty pleased about that. That's a real step up for me. So, this? You and me? I knew I didn't stand a chance the first time I laid eyes on you. You're too good to be true so how could it work? But, I gave it a shot anyway. You gotta give me credit for that. You know, that first night, I was hoping you might invite me in to talk — Seriously. Just to talk. That's all I wanted to do, because you seemed like someone who was easy to talk to, and maybe I could have made a case for myself — But, that didn't happen and I can see why. I mean, when a woman invites you in, it usually means there's at least a chance that sex will ensue right? And I can see why you wouldn't want to lead me in that direction, because that particular event is very special. You know what the most exciting part about making love to a woman is? For me, I mean? It's the fact that the woman would actually allow me to do it with her. And I'm not selling myself short here, don't get me wrong. I mean, I can hold up my end in the lovemaking department. No, I'm in there plugging all the way. But, to think that a woman would want to share something that intimate — that personal — with me . . . well, that thought excites me and satisfies me and fills my heart all at once, because that is such a wonderful gift. So, uh . . . *(He looks at his watch.)* Oh, boy. Look at the time. I've been rambling on like Rasputin. I'd better let you go. So, I guess this is good night then. And, uh . . . well . . . *(Andy leans in and gives Val a kiss on the cheek.)* It's been nice knowing you, Val. It's been very nice.

LOVELY DAY
Leslie Ayvazian

Dramatic
Martin, forties

> *Martin's son has been recruited for the military at his high school. His wife, a pacifist, is taking him and leaving. Here, Martin stands up to her.*

MARTIN: OK, OK, Fran. It's the language, OK, it's the language of a man who has just been told that his wife intends to leave with his son! You expect me to find the perfect phrase that allows you to feel, what, respected, you said?

. . . OK. I see. Then let me tell you how your words feel. First, you tell me that you have privately, secretly been concocting plans to escape. Is that the right word? Escape? Kidnap? No? Wrong? Both wrong? OK! Shall we stick with leave?! You are preparing to leave with our son . . . my son? You would leave? That's the word, Fran, would you agree? LEAVE? TAKE is another word. You are prepared to TAKE our son from his home and his life and put him somewhere where perhaps he'll . . . what? Compose? Music? Correct? That's what you said? Don't answer! Don't interrupt! And I said to you, you have overstepped! Yes! You have, Fran. You have absolutely overstepped! THE HELL WITH RESPECT. THAT'S THE TRUTH!

. . . That's the truth! And there's more. There's another word. Your word. Your word to me! Bully! You say that I use the language of a bully! I who have been a husband to the best of my ability. And a father to the best of my ability.

. . . And now, you say bully! Bully? You see me as a bully, Fran?! A BULLY! WHO IS THE BULLY HERE? *(Silence.)*

McREELE
Stephen Belber

Dramatic
Dar, mid-thirties, black

> *Darius McReele, on death row for sixteen years, has recently been*
> *exonerated because of a series of articles written by a white journalist.*
> *Here he is being interviewed on TV by Katya, who is also black.*

DAR: Every time a black person is "helped" by a white person, it shoves
the black person further into victim role, which only broadens the
problem. Not to mention it's an approach that has more to do with
white redemption than black reparation. It's lip service —
   . . . Because that kind of guilt-driven urge — as profoundly as
it might be felt — it takes away our power.
   . . . By killing our desire to live. I mean look at the average fe-
male welfare recipient: Poor, black, single teenage mother, the state
gives her housing, food stamps, health care, day care — no wonder
the girl doesn't get married, she's better off single. All she's gotta do
is make some babysitting money, borrow some cash and she's good
to go. All her energy goes into *finagling* instead of making a better
life —
   . . . It's the state that *engenders* it, Katya. It takes away her motivation.
   . . . I don't think that salt-and-pepper grad-school classes are
gonna make America run again. Your average black American does-
n't give a lick if Pfizer Drugs puts more black people on its board,
because at the end of the day — it's still Pfizer.
   . . . It's a matter of white people expecting from *us* the same things
they expect from their *own.* I mean would you really want *your* kid
going to Harvard just because someone felt *sorry* for her?
   . . . I'm saying we need to work *harder,* understand delayed grat-
ification, be responsible for our families. I'm not absolving the white
race; I'm just saying that the cycle of blame does no one any good.

. . . The answer starts with a question: How do we *re-imagine* the intervention? Making a difference is *more* than just some white kid losing his assembly-line job to a black kid. I'm talking money and energy needing to be redirected to the core. We need toilet paper and pencils in *grade* school a lot more than we need some high-yella black jerk in *law* school. There's like a 50 percent dropout rate for college-level affirmative action babies *anyway* because they're unprepared for what they face. *I* say legislate SAT prep courses in the ghettos, I say mandate a corporate matching donation to a *rec center* for every campaign contribution in this country. Require tobacco companies to replace all those nigger-aimed cigarette ads with billboards of Zora Neale Hurston quotes! Money where the mouth is, Katya, *that's* what I say!

McREELE
Stephen Belber

Dramatic
Dar, mid-thirties, black

> *Darius McReele, on death row for sixteen years, has recently been exonerated because of a series of articles written by a white journalist. He is a brilliant man, highly articulate, with deep political convictions, some of which he expresses here.*

DAR: The problem is that we make our decisions based on news obtained from corporate-owned media outlets. What we *need* is Ted Turner to finance a free-standing U.N. *media* division so that world crises receive air time *appropriate* to their level of trauma. That way, Palestinian refugee camps getting razed receive just as much air time as suicide bombers —

. . . I'm saying that Israeli lobbyists have more influence than Palestinian ones and that neither side should receive more news coverage than a two-week slaughter of a million people in Botswana.

. . . Our interest is in *humanity* —

. . . — it's calling for intervention based on *need* as opposed to self-interest. And if we can only peace-keep three times a year, we should choose based on empathy and care. Because human beings *care,* Gerry, and our political beliefs are *based* on that care. Read the Bill of Rights — it's why we *have* identity politics to begin with — because our Founding Fathers based this sucker on *humanist principles.* So when it comes to foreign policy we need to *follow* those principles. We need to ask ourselves, "What does that mean? — to be a *part* of the human race?" — independent of all *other* identity. What is it to be *human?*" And if it feels inherently *in*humane to sit back and watch people die in Botswana while millions get spent chasing oil, then *that's* where my politics will fall; before I'm American or black or an SUV driver. I'll vote how I'm *human.* Period. Because politics *does* go that deep.

McREELE
Stephen Belber

Dramatic
Dar, mid-thirties, black

> *Darius McReele, on death row for sixteen years, has recently been exonerated because of a series of articles written by a white journalist. He is a brilliant man, highly articulate, with deep political convictions. He is running for political office, and he is debating the incumbent on television who has questioned his story about what happened the night of the murder for which he was convicted.*

DAR: *(Honest as hell.)* You're right. I did nothing as Patrick was shot. I stood and did nothing. It was the most horrific, ugly moment of my life. Because I froze . . . and did nothing. *(Pause.)* One year to the date of that murder, I woke up and made three vows to myself: that I would tirelessly improve myself as a human being; that my last act before sleep each night would be a prayer for Patrick Cragen's family; and that I would spend the rest of my life working to ensure that kids like myself and Patrick no longer find themselves in situations like the one we were in that night. *(Pause.)* I have kept those vows, and I'll add to them right now, that if elected I will dedicate *every* ounce of my energy towards making a world where the look I saw in Patrick's eyes that night — the look of horror and pain and fear — *no longer exists.* Every ounce of my energy, Gerry. that's where I'll be coming from if elected. *(Pause.)* So until next week you can call me what you want, but that's my pledge — to Patrick's family, to the people of Delaware . . . to this nation.

McREELE
Stephen Belber

Dramatic
Rick, forties

> *Rick, a crusading journalist, has written a series of articles about
> what he believed was the wrongful murder conviction of a black man
> named Darius McReele, and these articles have helped to exonerate
> McReele, who has become a budding political figure. Rick has begun
> to wonder about the truth of what happened the night of the
> murder.*

RICK: *(Beat.)* Here's the thing, Darius. Opal told me she saw you shoot
Patrick that night. That she was walking down the block looking for
you and that she saw the three of you arguing and that she saw you
pick up Ronny's gun and shoot Cragen as he was fighting with Ronny.
(Pause.) That's what she says. *(Beat.)* And you should also know that
I visited Ronny in prison yesterday and spoke with him for an hour
and a half and he swore to me on a stack of bibles that *he* was the
one who shot Cragen. So here's my dilemma, Darius: I don't know
what to believe. I want very badly to believe what you're telling me.
I want it so bad I can't even tell you; but I also don't think that the
people of Delaware should elect as their senator a murderer. And as
a journalist, or a former journalist or *whatever* I am, I know this in-
formation needs to come out. It needs to come out. *(Pause.)* Because
otherwise you're gonna win this election next Tuesday and I'm still
not gonna know who you are.

MY DEAH
John Epperson

Comic
Coach, could be any age

> *My Deah is a Southern-fried gay spoof of Medea, set in Mississippi.*
> *The speaker is the local high school football coach.*

COACH: Today has brought out some secrets I would have preferred to hide.
And now I must admit that often when I sneak down to Mae's Cabaret, the Shantytown
Gay bar, I get involved in disputes, perhaps more impassioned
Than some think is fitting for a sports-minded fag-hound like me.
Though in fact athletic homosexuals can also have mental prowess.

Therefore, this is my reasoning: those people
Who don't have children
Enjoy the benefit in good fortune
Over those who do engage in parenthood.

Those yuppie breeders must wonder whether all their effort
Is spent for decent or worthless offspring.

I won't ever have a kid.
That's one less baby stroller, mowing
People down at the Dogwood Shopping Mall, y'all.
I'll never buy one of those goddamn strollers *(Suddenly turning to the house.)*
Cause I ain't interested no more in nothin' about any children!
That's the dang truth
Or my name ain't Coach Billy Joe McAllister the third!

Guess you better start lookin' for another job, Coach Billy Joe McAllister the third.

Maybe call up Miz Pepper and let her know you minored in runway modelin'.

(Coach sashays about and chants in a liberated but desperate manner.)

Billy Joe McAllister! Billy Joe McAllister! Linda Evangeleeesta! Linda Evangeleeesta!

'NAMI
Chad Beckim

Dramatic
Roachie, mid to late twenties

Roachie is speaking to his wife, Keesha. He has been caught attempting to sneak into his apartment after a rather embarrassing day during which he gambled, drank, and smoked the rent money Keesha had given to him.

ROACHIE: I woulda been heah like on time, 'cept I couldn't stop lookin' at tha moon. Yo, you shoulda seen it, baby. That shit was fuckin' amazin'! I was walkin' towards the buildin' an juss looked up and, boom! It was so ill. I had ta go up ta tha roof ta look at it. It was like, like the kinda moon you see in them movies 'bout California or the Wild West? Juss fuckin', huge an orange an so, so bright! An I'm sittin' there, all like, hypnotized an shit, juss starin' at it. An I started thinkin' of you — funniest shit, me lookin' at tha moon an thinkin' of you, knowin' you prolly waitin' for me in tha apartment, prolly heated at me — but I couldn't make myself leave. An then, like, boom, I remembered — tha only other time I evah saw tha moon look like that was tha night when we was at that club in Ozone? 'Member? Like, one of tha first times we evah went out-out, like on a date out? An that Dominican niggah came out his face at you, an I gave that niggah the beat-down of his life for disrespectin' you, an afterwards we was sittin' on some park bench, lookin' at tha moon an talkin'? You 'member that night? How tha moon was? I was up there, on tha roof, lookin' at tha moon an thinkin' of you, thinkin' how I should get you ta see it, an then, before I knew it, it like, went away or whutevah. Got all, normal an shit. I'm sorry you ain't see it, baby. That shit was hot. So thass where I been. *(Beat.)* Whah? Whah you lookin' at me like that for?

'NAMI
Chad Beckim

Dramatic
Harry, late thirties

Harry is speaking to his wife, Lil, who has become mentally unstable after a miscarriage. He has returned home to discover an Indonesian orphan in his bedroom, whom he believes his wife has kidnapped.

HARRY: You kidnapped her — do you realize that? You kidnapped a little girl and you're lying to me! Are you that broken that you don't realize that? Where the fuck did you get that little girl! Tell me!

. . . What is your defect — what are you thinking? *(Surrender.)* This is it. The end of it. Because I can't. I've spent the past six months taking care of you. Coddling you. Walking on eggshells so you wouldn't crumble into some pile of dust. Doing everything I could to make sure that you were getting better. Acting like a wet nurse for you, the same way your father does for your crazy fucking mother. For what? For nothing. It didn't make one bit of difference. Genetics finally caught up. And you. Sitting there. Wallowing in your own pity. Letting yourself waste away. Me thinking, "Tomorrow will be better. Tomorrow will be the day." And every single fucking day you slip further into oblivion. It hurts to look at you, Lil. You've become this horrible sideshow carnival version of yourself. I can't even look at you when you're knocked up. It's — you're . . . sick. *(Beat.)* I'm going to the police now. Going to inform them that my crazy fucking wife, who has spent the past two days pressing her ear to the fucking door listening for voices, prancing around the house in her wedding dress, ripping our walls apart — has finally cracked and abducted a little Chinese — sorry — Indonesian — girl. And I am going to watch as they strap your crazy fucking ass to a stretcher and cart you off to Bellevue. It ends. Now. Because this? You? Are worse than your mother. She's just imbalanced. But you? You are absolutely fucking crazy.

OFFICE SONATA
Andy Chmelko

Seriocomic
Lester, thirties to forties

> *For the past two weeks Lester, an Executive Vice President, has been
> toiling away in his office preparing for a presentation to clients from
> France. His temporary assistant, Meghan, has been in Los Angeles
> on an important audition. Lester doesn't think much of Meghan's
> pursuit of an acting career, and having her away at this important
> time has been very frustrating for him. When she returns, having
> failed to get the acting job, he unleashes a sarcastic tirade, one that
> he's been wanting to give ever since she began working for him.*

LESTER: You heard it here first everybody . . . MEGHAN ALTMAN BLEW
ANOTHER AUDITION!!! I mean really, I am shocked and appalled,
I was so sure that unlike your last . . . what are we up to now, ten
auditions? Twenty? A hundred? Well, I was SURE you'd get this one
right. So anyway now that we've covered that topic I'd love for you
to direct your attention back to the man responsible for paying your
bills, OK? I was very generous and gave you two weeks off, and now
we have clients coming in from France in a matter of days . . .
FRANCE! And if you were . . . and no one else is going to have the
guts to tell you this so you should be thankful for me . . . if you were
a good actress at all you would have no reason to be working here.
Someone would've discovered you a long time ago, honey. And deep
down you know that and that's why you keep coming back here and
doing what I tell you to. And I am telling you now to screw your
head on straight the way it belongs, and join us here in the REAL
WORLD! I spent an obscene amount of overtime while you were gone
preparing for this client meeting, and now it's your turn to roll up
your sleeves and pitch in. And God help you if I ever hear the word
"audition" out of your mouth again!

OVER THE TAVERN
Tom Dudzick

Comic
Rudy, twelve

Rudy performs his famous Ed Sullivan impression for his little brother Georgie.

RUDY: Wait'll you see this, Georgie! I just thought it up on the way home from school! *(Becomes an announcer.)* And now, ladies and gentlemen, live from New York, it's the *Ed Sullivan Show!*

. . . Tonight join Ed and his — quiet, Georgie — guests Gizelle McKenzie, Wayne and Shuster, Señor Wences, Tennessee Ernie Ford, and Ed's very special guest — Jesus Christ! And now, here he is, toast of the town, and syndicated columnist for the *New York Daily News* — Ed Sullivan!

(Ruddy turns his back to us, then faces front again as a stiff-necked, round-shouldered Ed Sullivan.)

Well, thank you, thank you, ladies and gentlemen. We have a r-r-really big shew for you tonight. But before we begin, out there in our audience is a lovely and talented nun. All the way from the seventh grade of Saint Casimir's Elementary School — let's have a nice hand for *Sister Clarisser!*

. . . You look lovely tonight, Sister. Now I don't want to say the good sister is old. But when Matthew, Mark, Luke, and John wrote the New Testament, who do you think corrected their spelling? . . . But on with our show. Here's my first guest tonight, all the way from Judear. Let's r-r-really hear it for a great guy, my pal — *Jesus Christ! Let's hear it!*

. . . Well, it's been a couple thousand years now and I'm looking down and what do I see? You know what I see? I'll tell you what I see. I see — *(Now angry, à la Ralph Kramden:)* — CATECHISM! Two hundred and fifty million nuns driving little kids crazy with rules,

rules, rules! Whackin' them over the knuckles with sticks! When did I say *this?!*

. . . That's the end, Georgie.

. . . You know what's great, Georgie? Nobody knows what Jesus really sounded like, so my imitation could be perfect!

A PICASSO
Jeffrey Hatcher

Dramatic
Picasso, fifties

> *The great artist Pablo Picasso is speaking to Miss Fischer, a "cultural attaché" for the Nazis who have recently occupied Paris. The Germans have three Picassos they have stolen, but they have reason to believe they are fakes. Miss Fischer is trying to get authentications from Picasso. Here he is ranting about Guillaume Apollinaire, who claimed to have "discovered" him.*

PICASSO: *(Claps his hands to begin.)* This is the story of a critic, so let me tell it the way a critic might. *(Assumes a lecturing demeanor.)* Picasso, the boy painter left his native Spain and moved north, to Paris. Where he paints and starves and fucks. He sells some paintings here and there. He meets Gertrude Stein. He knows Gertrude Stein before she meets Alice, that is how long ago this is. He agrees to paint her portrait. It takes forever. When her portrait is finished, she says to Picasso: "I don't look like that!" Picasso says to her: "You will." And she does. Picasso is *surviving* in Paris . . . but he needs to make a break, make his reputation, put himself above the rest. Enter Guillaume Apollinaire. A critic. Brilliant. Charming. Polish, a big Pole from Warsaw — queer — but in the snob hierarchy of Paris, he fits in. Picasso is not always so comfortable. To the world he is becoming "Picasso," but to himself, he is still a little bit Pablito Ruiz. Picasso invites him up to see his work . . . and it is like the beginning of a love affair . . . Picasso paints. Apollinaire writes about it. Apollinaire theorizes. Picasso makes it real. In and out of each other's rooms, arguing in cafes day and night, if Picasso can be said to have a second self, it is Apollinaire. Apollinaire loves Picasso. Loves Picasso; so much so, he is his champion. And when Picasso finally becomes well-known, Apollinaire has a tendency to tell people he "discovered" him. But you know . . . there is always a resentment the discovered has for the discoverer. Always going around saying, "I found you, I made you." Fuck you! I made myself!

POKER AND THE DECLARATION OF THE RIGHTS OF MAN

Jesse Kellerman

Seriocomic
Chuck, thirty to fifty

> *Chuck is trying to convince his friend Phil to expel his wife from their weekly poker game. Chuck doesn't think poker and women should mix; plus he is losing big time to Phil's wife.*

CHUCK: You have got to stop her. She is going to ruin you, my friend, and there is nothing I can do about it, because I play for keeps. I am not going to give this back, Phil! This is my earnings, and this is my God-given right! And she is trampling all over the rights of all men ever'where, and it is encumbered upon you to make sure she don't. That is your responsibility. As a man. And as an *American. (Pause. He jumps to his feet.)* For the love of God, Phil! Do something! This is a matter of *rights!* And I am not talking property rights here, like who owns what or who gets to piss in what corner of the field, or whatnot. All men! Ever'where! They're all lookin' towards you, Philly, saying, "Is that boy a man, or a boy? Is he going to hold up the rights of every man in this blessed country to play poker without the illogical and irresponsible intrusions of his wife and all other raging, pre-menstruating females? Or is he going to be the feckless whippin-boy of some ladyfingered, bathroom-frequenting, poker-destroying woman with his balls in a vice?" *(Pause.)* Answer me, Phil. And bear in mind that you are answering for all men all across this land. *(Pause.)*

POST-OEDIPUS
Steven Gridley

Dramatic
Eteocles, twenty to forty

> *After the fall of Oedipus his two sons Eteocles and Polyneices agreed to be co-rulers of Thebes, alternating rule in seven-year terms; but after his seven years were up Eteocles refused to relinquish the throne. Before a jury, here Eteocles is responding to Polyneices' charge that he has unjustly stolen the throne.*

ETEOCLES: Plain and true. Well done, Polyneices.
> *(He takes a moment to prepare.)*

Equality and fairness. Equality and fairness is the common plea of the ignorant and simpleminded who are unable to grasp the single undeniable fact about our existence: that men are created unequal and treated unfairly, and that the Gods take pleasure in our pain. In truth, equality and fairness have no existence in this world beyond the name which my brother beautifully invokes plain and true. Well done, Polyneices. But I ask, where in nature does equality exist? Nowhere. Lions have claws. Lambs don't. It's not fair. But the Gods in their infinite wisdom saw fit to create such a world. Who am I to unmake what they have made? To do so would be to risk punishment because, yes, it's true, justice and fairness carry with them a penalty. My father was just and fair and wise. What was his reward? A big pile of steamy shit. Is that just? No, it isn't. Am I bitter? No, I'm not. You know why? Because that's life. But Polyneices, plain and true, cries unfair about his stewardship, the self-same stewardship I plainly outsmarted him in acquiring. I am a lion. He's a lamb. Anybody stupid enough to actually agree to give his country away does not have what it takes to be king. Should I feel guilty for having claws when my brother clearly only has wool? Let my lambish brother cuddle himself at night with his warm feelings of fairness and equality. I, however, am a king and kings must keep their hearts cold.

THE RADIANT ABYSS
Angus MacLachlan

Dramatic
Steve Enloe, twenty-three

> *Steve Enloe is a nighttime security guard for a property-management office run by Erin Skidmore out of a local mall. A wacko religious group has moved in next door to Erin's office, and she wants them out, so she has seduced Steve Enloe, her former "sex-puppy" into trying to help her get rid of them. Here Steve Enloe is talking to Erin.*

STEVE ENLOE: What's up your butt? I went. I wasn't supposed to be there, so, I "broke in." Same difference. And it was eerie, man — But then — I lucked out. I found those collection plates in this back cabinet — not locked up or anything — how lame is that? So I grabbed some of that shit . . .

. . . And then I *just* start to tear down this banner, these big banners they have, when — I don't know if it was the Orkin or the flu or what — but I threw up.

. . . Right beside the altar. I just started puking like a motherfucker. Like the smoothie and the General Chow chicken I had at the mall, and it kept going till I just dry heaved for like half an hour! It was the worst, man. I felt like I was dying. I hate throwing up. I'd *rather* die . . . So then — I laid down on my back and I just started to look around. And it was weird 'cause it really looks like a *real* church in there. All these signs that say "God Is Great Love." And "We are one people" and it felt like a church, you know? Quiet . . . And as I was laying there I thought — shit — what the fuck am I doing here? . . . You know? . . . It just came to me. I don't know anything about these people . . . And then I thought about what you said, Ina: What was this shit I was pulling supposed to do, really? Make them stop believing in what they believe in? . . . I don't even know what they believe in. I only know what Erin tells me . . . So they got a van, so what. You know? It just hit me. Hard . . . It was really stupid. The whole deal. It was bogus . . . So . . . I got the hell out of there.

SEE ROCK CITY
Arlene Hutton

Comic
Raleigh, twenties

> *This play is set toward the end of World War II. Raleigh has a medical condition that has kept him from military service and from working. He is trying to be a writer while his wife May supports them. Here he is telling an amusing story to May.*

RALEIGH: 'Member how he had that ole white mule? That ole white mule and a buckboard?

. . . 'Member how Dimwit used to meet the train every day and carry people's luggage? He'd sit on the bench outside Stewie's, napping. That ole mule in the back, hitched to the buckboard? That mule would know exactly what time it was and just before the train was due would come 'round to the front of Stewie's and stand there in front of Dimwit Danny waitin' to go to the station and meet the train.

. . . That mule would stay in the back lot behind the store until he knew it was time to go meet the train.

. . . Well, one day, I take a bucket of black paint and a paintbrush and while Dimwit Danny is nappin' in out front of Stewie's I go around t' the back and paint black stripes on that ole white mule.

. . . Wanted to see what a zebra looked like.

. . . In school we're reading all about Africa and I can't figure out what a zebra would look like. So I paint stripes on that ol' mule and then I stand back and look at it and I say to myself, well, so that's what a zebra looks like!

. . . And my momma nearly whupped me for it.

. . . Well, about the time I finish paintin' stripes on him, the mule knows it's time to wake up Dimwit to go meet the train, so that striped mule takes off headin' 'round to the front of Stewie's. And I follow after him because I want to imagine what a *moving* zebra looks like, with the stripes moving an' all. And ever'body on Main Street stops in their tracks when they see this zebra-striped mule and they laugh and point and laugh and Dimwit just can't figure out how his mule has stripes all of a sudden. Somebody sees me with the paint bucket and runs and tells my daddy. Well, after supper my momma takes me to Dimwit's house — he lived with his sister — and my momma drags me up the steps and knocks on the door. When Dimwit opens it, my momma tells him that I have somethin' to say to him. So I tell Dimwit how I painted stripes on his mule because I wanted to see what a zebra looked like and that my momma is gonna whoop me for it. And Dimwit, he looks at me, and then he looks at my momma and he says to my momma that I didn't mean no harm. And for her not to punish me. And my momma has to promise that she won't lay a hand on me.

SMOKE ON THE MOUNTAIN HOMECOMING

Connie Ray and Alan Bailey

Dramatic
Stanley, forties

> *This is a musical about a family of Gospel singers. All are devout,
> but Stanley has had a lot of difficulty in his life staying on the straight-
> and-narrow path. During the show, the Sanders family members
> testify about their faith. This is Stanley's statement.*

STANLEY: When Jesus Christ came upon Peter by the Sea of Galilee, He
said, "Throw down your nets and follow me." Peter said, "Beats fish-
ing," quit his job, and took off for parts unknown. That's me.

When Jesus walked on the water, the rest were afraid. Peter said,
"I can do that," but after the first few steps, his faith flew out from
under him and he sank like a stone. That's me. When Christ gath-
ered the disciples and explained that He would be rejected, killed,
and rise again, Peter pulled Christ to one side and said, "Buddy, I
think I can help you with your story." That's me.

When Jesus warned Peter that Satan was looking to sift him like
wheat, Peter said, "No, Lord, I love you so much I would die for you."
But three times before the sun rose, Peter swore he'd never met the
man. That's me.

Peter was a drifter, a hothead, a know-it-all. He made promises
and broke 'em, started things he couldn't finish, made messes he
couldn't clean up. But Jesus forgave him, loved him, saved him. *(Mo-
tioning to Pastor Oglethorpe.)* That's him. Your Reverend Oglethorpe
sat with me last night at the Blue Nose Tavern. And where everyone
else sees nothing but a lost cause, Mervin took the chance to spread
a little grace.

Last time I was here, I had left the family and gone out singing
on my own 'cause I was better than them and they were holding me
back. Last time I was here, I was in the movies, but I quit 'cause I

got better things to do than stand around and wait for Gene Autry. Last time I was here, I was making records, but some man in a tie wanted to tell me what to sing, and nobody tells me what to do. Last time I was here, I was on the bill with the big-name groups, but management and I didn't see eye-to-eye and they got tired of bailing me out. 'Cause, you know, there's a Blue Nose Tavern in every little town.

Now I play where they'll have me and I sing what they want. Travelling songs, courtin' songs, I-done-wrong songs, and I-been-done-wrong songs. But they don't want to hear gospel songs. 'Cause gospel songs make them remember, and the men hang their heads and the women cry.

Sometimes it's not a big thing that knocks you down. How many times have I started over? How many chances have I lost? Always saying tomorrow. Tomorrow I'll do better. But I don't. *(Laughing.)* Have you heard the one about the preacher who walked into a bar? Mervin about cleared the place out last night. You've never seen so much ducking and tiptoeing. Some flat-out scorched a path to the door. *(To Pastor Oglethorpe.)* I bet Luther's sorry he called you, you hurt his business so bad. *(To congregation.)* I'd have run, too, but the boy's bald-faced grit caught me by the coattails. Old Mervin here pulled up a chair, ordered up an Orange Crush, shelled a few peanuts, and told me stories about that rascal Peter.

Ever since the war ended, something's been pulling me back here hard. This last month I've been all through these parts, dodging and weaseling around trying to make it all the way home. I tangled with it all day today and determined to head back for parts west.

But I came here. If Peter messed up that bad and our Savior still asked him to look after his sheep, maybe there's a prayer for me.

SPATTER PATTERN
Neal Bell

Dramatic
Tate, mid-forties

> *Tate is a college professor. A gruesome murder has been committed.*
> *Tate is a suspect. Here, he responds to his wife, Ellen, who has asked*
> *him if he did it.*

TATE: It's a poser. I was thinking you.
     . . . Because you were getting old.
     Because you thought I was fucking around.
     Because *you* fucked around — to get even with me —
     and only got lonelier.
     Because you used to stand outside my office,
     with your ear to the door —
     and there were times when you didn't hear a thing,
     and you'd remember how, when I went down on you,
     you were quiet, biting your lip, not making a sound,
     like you didn't want me to know what I was doing to you . . .

(He makes the sound of his wife's low moan, she flinches.)

     This student you were jealous of — Ms. Andrea Evans —
     the dead one?
     She was comparing America, today, to Nazi Germany.
     I told her — to her great irritation —
     I found her analogies facile.
     I'd explain why —
     and she'd think about it. In silence.
     Ellen, that's all you heard:
     a silence you couldn't understand.
     So you found a knife — the one I thought I'd lost, from my
days in the service —

and you stood in the dark of an alley,
wondering how your life had come down to this —
and when my student walked by, you grabbed her.
And opened her up to the elements.

STRAIGHT ON TIL MORNING
Trish Harnetiaux

Seriocomic
Friendly, sixties

> *Friendly is a very outgoing bartender, a meat-and-potatoes sort of guy. Here he is talking to a customer about the rapid gentrification the Brooklyn neighborhood he grew up in has been undergoing, and how that's been good for business.*

FRIENDLY: That place? Down on Kent? Used to be New York's first all black topless bar. They're tryin' to rent it out as an apartment now. They'll rent out anythin' at this point. Can only imagine what sort of stories they're spinnin' to jack up the price, just talk to Hoard, he owns it. He's probably sayin' Harriet Tubman herself used to woo the crowds. Funny thing is you dig two feet down in the backyard and strike oil — and not the fancy Texas kind. Biggest spill ever back in the seventies — millions and millions of gallons oozing below the surface. No Joke.

Hoard? He's got his Real Estate office over on Graham, considers himself a "developer" now, whatever that means. He needs to take it easy, starting to throw around a bunch of ten-dollar words, getting a bit hard on the ears if you know what I mean.

Yeah, I'm on top of all that pool talk too. Well Hoard's got a forty-year grudge festerin' there, his hand and all. He wants to put up some sorta skyscraper. But the kids — they want to turn it into some kind of concert place, some kind of a *festa*. I'm not taking sides. It used to be immaculate. Tended to your every need. You needed a towel? They had towels. And they were handed to you by a pretty lady. Another era. *Che Peccato.*

Yeah, it's been changin'. Still changin' some say. They all started movin' in about ten, fifteen years ago. Word was the village had spread as far east as it could get and prices were driving them artists over the bridge. I don't mind too much, shoved the Hasids down some which they're not happy about, concentrated most of the Poles nicely past the park, didn't bother us Italians really, we've pretty much kept our hold on the immediate area, and them Latins always had their Southside. More people like yourself though coming in asking questions all the time.

Last few years has breathed some new life in this place. I am now a condo owner in the sunny state of Florida. No Joke.

We don't o-ffici-ally open for another hour, but can I buy ya a drink?

STRAIGHT ON TIL MORNING

Trish Harnetiaux

Dramatic
Hoard, fifties

> *Hoard is a first-generation Brooklynite, descended from Polish im-*
> *migrants. He has built his real estate business from the ground up*
> *and the gentrification of the neighborhood recently has been very prof-*
> *itable for him. Here he is in his office talking on the telephone with*
> *a potential development partner. His sights are set on a jewel of a*
> *site, an enormous abandoned pool. He needs a solid, but silent,*
> *partner.*

HOARD: You stopped by Ships Mast huh? Good man Friendly. Born and
bred on that very block. He's family. Someone that's makin' a pretty
penny off the neighborhood boom.

Have you seen it yet? The last untouched, wide open space in
the neighborhood. An entire city block. Back in the day that pool
could hold more than six-thousand eight-hundred people. It's enormous. When I think about that much space, and what I could do
with it vertically . . .

I could easily fit four buildings with ten, maybe twelve units per
floor. Sky's the limit on floors. We're talking about eight hundred
dollars a square foot and me waving good-bye through the back window of my Little Red Corvette. That's right — condos.

I'll leave a bit of room for some sort of something that benefits
the neighborhood. It'll be a write-off.

The way I'm looking at it, the yuppies'll be over there in no time.
And we'll be following the next artist trail.

I need one solid partner in the venture. A silent partner if you
know what I mean. The locals don't mind a neighborhood guy makin'
a little noise — but you — you might scare 'em off to be honest.
I've takin' the liberty of havin' some blueprints drawn up, nothing

formal, you know — rough sketches of how I see it. Sure — you can see them, I'll be at the bar later. Let's say five o'clock?

Yeah, I made the offer last night at the council meeting — went face-to-face with some pathetic petition from a bunch of pain-in-the-ass artist types. They wanna do some concert or something. Nothing to worry about. I laid it out to them — and they were all there — the Polish Alliance, Friends of Greenpoint, McCarren Park Conservancy, the Soccer Association, the Bocci ball guys, goddamn *Alcoholics Anonymous* was there. I showed 'em how they could use the money to better more prized projects of the neighborhood. Build 'em a new statue or somethin'. Neighborhood loves its statues. OK, see ya later.

STRAIGHT ON TIL MORNING
Trish Harnetiaux

Dramatic
Price, forties

> *Price, a professor at a small liberal arts college, has come to Brooklyn to find his nephew Peter. Here he tells Peter of a dream he had in which Michael — Peter's brother, who drowned many years ago— has come back to visit, unaware that he is dead.*

PRICE: Night before last I had a dream. It's the day after Michael died. I'm home and the doorbell rings. I answer it and standing in front of me is Michael . . . white and puffy from all the water. He's wearing that old green Springsteen shirt.

. . . I freeze, just stare at him. He walks in laughing and talking about how he'd just been swimming and how he didn't know why he'd been such a baby about water all these years and how *he'd just loved it.* "Had a blast Price, an adventure." He walks into the living room, sits down on the carpet and pulls out his bag of marbles.

We started playing . . . Then I realize . . . *he does not know that he has died.* And I can't tell him. He stays for a year.

. . . We don't leave the house once. And no one comes to look for us. As the date that Michael drowned starts coming up again, he begins to act strange. More sullen and withdrawn. Like he knows what's coming and that it's going to happen again. I don't know what to do. The night before the anniversary of his drowning Michael sits silent. I can't get him to speak. He lays beside me, holding on to just my index finger — doesn't let go. Just before dawn he gets up and walks to the front door. I follow him. He leaves the house and walks down to the lake. I somehow know, in the dream, that I can't do anything, that I can't stop him. And he walks into the water. He walks in so peacefully, the water is so calm. And then . . . he's gone, and I wake up.

STRAIGHT ON TIL MORNING

Trish Harnetiaux

Dramatic
Peter, twenties

> *Peter is a scout for a hot new record label. He is very charismatic,*
> *oozing with charm and self-confidence. He has not spoken to his fam-*
> *ily for ten years. Here, he tells his uncle about the one time he dared*
> *to dream of returning home and why he eventually decided he could*
> *never go home again.*

PETER: What am I going to do in Connecticut? Start a *family*? Buy a house?
Become a scholar like you? Fish? This, right here, is where I belong.
My community. What a horrible word, *community*.

. . . Look, I tried to go back once. This notion had come to
me — I want to say in a dream, but I think I might have been awake.
I'd go back at night — sneak through the open window to my room,
then curl up in bed as though I'd never left. She'd find me in the
morning and she'd let out a cry that would break your fuckin' heart.
Her famous boy had returned — and she'd look ten years younger
and happy — maybe more proud — she'd throw on her best dress
and insist on taking me all around, show me off. I even got my hair
cut at Jinny's the night before — she cuts Luna Eclipse's hair. All
spiked and messy and important. *(Grabs the bottle, taking a huge swig.)*
And I was almost at the door, knob in hand, chain off, and the truth
just . . . hit. Pummeled really. I wasn't *anything. (This is the weakest
we ever see Peter.)* I was thinking how it was all *just* about to change.
How I was like this early Quincy Jones — before Michael
Jackson — and would be worth millions one day. But, for now, I
was just *Peter*. And she'd probably be pissed I hadn't called. Pissed I
hadn't become a doctor or whatever the fuck Michael had wanted
to be. So, I threw down my bag and went to meet Isabele for a drink

at Ship's Mast. Friendly was working and that seemed about as close to home as I was going to get. People know me here.

. . . Here. In the neighborhood. They see me and they want to talk to me. They know that *I know.*

TROUT STANLEY
Claudia Dey

Seriocomic
Trout, thirties

> *Trout is a mysterious drifter who has shown up in a northern Cana-*
> *dian town. He claims to be looking for the lake where his parents*
> *drowned, but he may also be responsible for the disappearance of a*
> *local stripper and Scrabble champ. Here he is talking to Sugar, an*
> *agoraphobic young woman, who is attracted to this strange and mys-*
> *terious man.*

TROUT: I have a foot fetish.

. . . An' a slight drinkin' problem.

. . . I believe in kissing. For weeks at a time. I believe in the un-charted territories of the human brain an' I am against the monar-chy. I believe that comin' of age is man's cruellest invention. I believe that forgiveness is overrated. I believe in time travel an' space travel. I believe that cooking is an act of love. I believe in revenge as much as I believe in peace. I believe that the divine is where solitude and togetherness meet in perfect seamless harmonious union. I believe in undying loyalty. I believe that war is a godly trick forcing us to look into the weakest parts of bein' human. An' I believe that our great tragedy is that we haven't thought to look. I believe that the nipple, the tongue, the lips, the place where the ear meets the neck, our eye-lashes, as well as our sensual parts, are nature's most gracious offer-ings. I believe in fragility, slowness an' the long way around. I believe that the soul has a taste, a color an' a smell, an' I believe that the soul can have orgasms. I believe that we're all animals, an' that anything worth anything comes from the beast within.

TROUT STANLEY
Claudia Dey

Seriocomic
Trout, thirties

> *Trout is a mysterious drifter who has shown up in a northern Cana-*
> *dian town. He claims to be looking for the lake where his parents*
> *drowned, but he may also be responsible for the disappearance of a*
> *local stripper and Scrabble champ. Here he is talking to Grace, who*
> *cares for her agoraphobic sister Sugar and runs the town dump, who*
> *has wondered if he is responsible for the disappearance of the strip-*
> *per, and who sees him as a threat because he claims to be in love*
> *with Sugar, whom he has just met.*

TROUT: I don't know. This is my point: I don't know anything. Let me
tell ya how this looks from my end, Lion Queen. We have been walkin'
for years. Penniless mutes, failed visionaries. Tryin' to get home.
We have met every kind o' human face. Almos' there, we're tired. We're
thirsty. We need to catch our breath. We stumble onto this place; it's
the only one aroun'. We peer in the window thinkin' maybe the folk
who live here'll put us up, feed us sausages and lend us their bath-
water. Maybe we'll feel comfort. Sometimes, all a man wants is comfort.

But no. I'm in eternal love. I'm at a birthday party. I'm bein' tied
up. I'm bein' kissed. I'm bein' held hostage, at gunpoint, by my Sugar's
twin — who, by the way, looks nothin' froggin' like her. All fair game.
It's an unpredictable universe, I know that. But then I'm bein' accused
o' murder. Now this is uncalled for. I would never harm a woman so
long as my blood signature is Trout Stanley.

But I don't think that's your concern Grace Ducharme. That's
just a decoy, the huntress' ceramic birdie, the Lion Queen's trick call.
Pow pow. You're shootin' the sky. Well, here's what's fallin' from it:
Love. Love makes us, period.

This lowest on the chain o' life, this bottom-feedin' fish, this mistake has one miracle, an' that one miracle is my love for Sugar Ducharme. Bull's-eye. Shoot me dead an' even then we'll be together. That is why, Grace Ducharme, that is why I cannot lie, that is why I cannot tell you that.

UNCLE JACK
Jeff Cohen

Seriocomic
Jack, fifty

> *This play is a contemporary version of* Uncle Vanya, *set in Appalachia. Here, Jack (the Vanya character) is ranting to Dr. Michael Ashe about the arrival of his nemesis, Professor Alexander Coughlan, whose late first wife was Jack's sister and who has recently remarried.*

JACK: EXACTLY! He bought twenty cases of paper from the Office Depot in Morgantown, they delivered it in a semi for crissakes. That's fifty reams a carton. That's five hundred sheets a ream. That's five hundred thousand pieces of paper! That's what's killing your beloved forests, Michael! And for what? Nothing! He should forget the art crap and just write his autobiography. What a phenomenon that would be! He'd sell three copies at least. How would it go — a retired professor. No, not graphic enough. Here we go — a phlegmatic old fossil A dried-up fish. I like that. A sort of stuffed academic old trout. Groaning and grumbling incessantly about his arthritis and his liver and his rheumatism and his phlebitis. But that's just hypochondria. What's really eating at him is envy. Envy! And frustration that anyone in the know knows what a dried-up old hack he really is! So how did he get here in the first place? Here's the setup: He lives on income from the estate of his first wife that gives him his New York City lifestyle that enabled him to entrap his gorgeous child of a second wife. And then he moves back here to live, second wife in tow, with the first wife's family — and his daughter that he hasn't given a crap about in a good fifteen years. And it's not like he *wanted* to move back here. Oh no — he's such a nothing that he couldn't afford to stay in New York after Columbia gave him the boot! This ass is forever moaning about what a bad shake life has given him when the fact is he's the single luckiest man in the goddamn world! This reptile hit the jackpot. Just think about it: Who was the sonuvabitch before he turned his Don Juan oil charm on my poor kid sister? A nobody, that's who. Lehigh University for crissakes! But then he seduces my sister, marries into my family, and suddenly he's the son-in-law of a senator. Now, lo and behold, academic degrees are conferred upon him like ribbons on a fat sow at a state fair. Professor at Columbia University for crissakes? Using *my* daddy's name to make his good-for-nothing way in the world. But you know what, Michael?

. . . None of it matters.

. . . Because luck is no substitute for talent. And of that little item our Professor Fish is singularly bereft. For twenty-five years the man's been lecturing and writing about art which just happens to be a subject he knows nothing about. For twenty-five years he's been riding the backs of the dealers and the poseurs and the investors like a jockey on a nag, writing with all the integrity of a racing form tout at the track, chewing over other people's ideas, spouting off with his thesaurus about Modernism, Post Modernism, Post Post Modern Modernism and any other goddamn label he can attach to that swill and the *Village Voice* prints it and Mother dutifully keeps his scrapbook and for twenty-five years he's been lecturing and writing about the kind of crap that no intelligent person would ever take seriously and which ninety-nine point nine nine nine percent of the world couldn't give a good goddamn about anyway!!! Twenty-five years of chasing his own shadow, primping in his own goddamn mirror, building himself up in his own mind to excel at the one thing he does better than anybody else on earth which is his own goddamn, presumptuous, condescending, narcissistic ARROGANCE! And now, when it's all said and done, the truth comes out at last, the truth that Alexander Coughlan has to run all the way to the hills of West Virginia to avoid — he's a nobody. A nothing. Absolute. Utter. Obscure. Failure. Who cares about him, Michael? Who cares? NOBODY does! Strutting around like a goddamn peacock for twenty-five years, living off the fruit of *my* daddy's reputation, living off the fruit of *my* labor! And now, at the moment of truth, now when it's all come crashing down and he comes yelping up to my front door with his tail between his legs, do you wanna know what *really* burns me up?

    . . . The bastard won't even admit to it!!! We still have to run around playing his little game. He struts around here like God Almighty Himself and expects us to bend and kneel and genuflect in his presence! Talk about CHUTZPAH!

UNCLE JACK
Jeff Cohen

Seriocomic
Jack, fifty

> *This play is a contemporary version of* Uncle Vanya, *set in Appalachia. Here Jack Vaughan (the Vanya character) is speaking to his niece Sophie, Helena, Dr. Ashe, and others. Jack is making fun of Sophie's defense of what he feels to be Dr. Ashe's ridiculous crusade to save the forests of West Virginia.*

JACK: Yeah! Yeah! Hooray! Everyone — loud cheers for the sentiments of my love-struck niece! It's a fact: Trailer-park Appalachian men never mistreat their trailer-park Appalachian women. It's just Knights of the Round Table and Damsels wearing silk! Jerry Springer didn't make his goddamn fortune on the hysterics of Wall Street bankers for Christ's sake!

. . . — Good Lord, Sophie! How can you bring that load of crap in here with a straight face? I used to think you were a pretty smart cookie. Oh well. I guess *love* has turned you all mushy and romantic. Now don't look at me like that. Michael — at least you have to admit how ridiculous that all sounds. There's not a shred of nobility left in the whole goddamn world that hasn't been co-opted by marketers and pitchmen. The Hard Rock Cafe, I understand, has an electronic display counting down the vanishing acres of the world's rain forests. *The Hard Rock Cafe!!!* Rain-forest destruction as some corporate marketing maven's ploy to sell more twenty-five-dollar cheeseburgers and seventy-five-dollar T-shirts. Cheeseburgers, by the way, made from the slaughtered cattle of stockyards whose pens and pastures have been carved out of the bulldozing of thousands of acres of South American rain forests! T-shirts made off the back-breaking sweat of a million Chinese children in concentration camps all over Asia. Hoo-fucking-ray! *(Adopting a hillbilly accent.)* Y'ask me, the whole goddamn state o' West Virginny oughta clear cut every last tree, twig, and stick o' woods, oughta level every last hill, an' just sell the land off t'the highest bidder! Build some more chemical plants! Set up some more o' them toxic dumps! Kill a coupla thousand more o' them dad-burned coal miners makin' bigger profits for them kind-hearted folks at Big Coal and Energy! They ain't enuf new golf courses 'round here! They ain't enuf Coal Industry lobbyists givin' enuf money to them EPA fellas over there in Washington Dee Cee! Hell yeah! That's my solution for balancin' the goddamn budget and winnin' the war agin them Moslem Ay-Rab rag-head terrorists! Sell the whole fuckin' state fer all I care! But you liberal whackos hate America! You Greeny whackos hate Jeesus!! You jest want to tax an' spend me to my grave — jest so you can save a few goddamn trees!!!!

UNCLE JACK
Jeff Cohen

Seriocomic
Dr. Michael Ashe, fifty, African-American

This play is a contemporary version of Uncle Vanya, *set in Appalachia. Dr. Ashe is an environmentalist who is devoted to saving the forests of West Virginia. Here he responds to his friend Jack's suggestion that the forests should be cut down for profit.*

ASHE: See, that's what I love about this guy. He loves to test my good nature. Loves to get my goat. Fact is, if I thought he was serious for one second I'd buy myself a shotgun and shoot him in the head. Here's what I *will* tell you — twenty years from now these forests that make this view so picturesque, these forests may be gone. Every single day thousands of acres, millions of trees perish under the axe, get buried under the bulldozer. Sophie's right, these forests are the oxygen of the planet, they are our lungs, they are the air that we breathe. Without them, what do you think will happen? Go ahead, make yourself feel superior by thinking I'm a crackpot. I'm not. This is all well-documented science. Entire populations of birds and animals are being wiped out by the wholesale destruction. And for what? For a buck? I'm telling you this is a holocaust of enormous proportions and repercussions but it means no more to the Jack Vaughns of the world than a series of sophomoric jokes that make more of a goddamn idiot out of you, my friend, than me! All your cynical, smarmy little jokes ain't worth *shit,* Jack! What I do by planting a stand of young trees or helping the forest rangers with whatever they need me to do may be insignificant against the onslaught — but at least *I DO SOMETHING!* And what I'm trying to tell you is that if we *ALL DO SOMETHING,* then there's at least a hope that *SOMETHING GETS DONE!* So I get on my pulpit and I demand that *every last one of us DO something* positive and heroic. Good Christ, what is happening to this planet is so monumentally *STUPID!* Jack Vaughn, you and your smug, smirking kind are a paradigm of monumental stupidity! *YOU, my friend, ARE the problem!* You love laughing at the destruction of everything around you, you love tearing down anything that's good and decent, because you are an unhappy man who has to make sure that everyone else is just as unhappy as *he is! (A beat.)* I want everyone to look at Jack Vaughn, look at that ugly little grin on his face. He thinks that to see me flying off the handle is an accomplishment, that that is somehow worthwhile. But then you wouldn't dare take anything seriously, would you? I'll shut up now. I've probably said too much that I'll regret later. You now have ample evidence that I am, in fact, off my rocker. But I'll leave you with this. When I walk through the forest, when I see and smell and touch the sun-dappled trees that I helped to save and raise and nourish, it makes me feel good about myself. Unlike Jack, I don't feel as though my life is wasted. I have to think that a thousand years from now people will still be able to enjoy the magnificence of this planet and I will have made a contribution to that. That is my raison d'être and my little bit of immortality. Helena, I hope that someday you can feel something like the deep satisfaction I get when I plant a fir or an oak or a maple. The cool black earth. The slender branches. The smell of living wood.

UNCLE JACK
Jeff Cohen

Seriocomic
Jack, fifty

> *This play is a contemporary version of* Uncle Vanya, *set in Appalachia. Jack (the Vanya character) cannot believe that the stunningly beautiful Helena, with whom he is in love, has thrown her life away by marrying boring old Professor Coughlan.*

JACK: "I liked you then." Why did I wait? I had my chance. She just said it. I could've asked her out, to dinner, to a play. Good God. We'd have strolled around the fountain at Lincoln Center. Or watched the ice skaters at Rockefeller Center. Or just stood in Central Park by the Sheep Meadow looking at the magnificent skyline of Midtown Manhattan. I would have kissed her. And she would have melted against me. I knew she liked me. Just didn't have the guts to do anything about it. We'd be married now. beside each other in bed. We'd wake up from the crackle of the thunder and we'd watch the lightning and we'd cuddle together. Begin to touch one another. Without a word we'd begin to kiss. She would brush her lips against my ear and whisper to me how much she loved me and how happy she was that I had taken her out all those years ago when I was visiting New York and the sound of her whispered voice would be music sweeter than Mozart. *(A pause.)* But let's take a reality check, Jack old boy. It didn't happen. And here you are. And now it is over, done — he's got her and you are finished. God, what has happened? How could it all go so wrong? How dare she say that to me! I'd rather she said she *never* liked me. I *hate* her for saying that to me. That's the reward I get for being serious for one fucking moment! That's it Her motherfucking patronizing arrogant pity? WELL FUCK YOU! FUCK YOU!! FUCK YOU!!! And him! I used to think the world of him too, she's right about that. I'd go to New York City with these fucking naïve stars in my eyes fantasizing on the plane about how Alexander was going to rescue me from this shitty little life I live out here. I'd send him his money every goddamn month and convinced myself it was an *investment!* Sophie and I working like fucking dogs to squeeze every last penny from this place so that he could live his important lifestyle hobnobbing with the rich and famous and *someday I would join him!* He'd take me around to publishers and literary agents. The motherfucker was going to open doors for me and they would recognize that I was brilliant and he said he would and I believed him! And then, suddenly, he just retires! Just like that, he says he's fed up with the city and he's going to spend the rest of his miserable life leeching off us here! And just as suddenly I knew. I fucking knew. I knew what I damn well should have known twenty goddamn years ago — it was all a lie! All bullshit! Get *me* published? He can't even get *himself* published, the goddamn fake — goddamn phony! YOU ARE NOTHING!!!! He's nothing. An abject failure who preyed on Sophie and Mother and me as slick as a grifter. And we were the dupes. God, how can I be such an idiot? Well FUCK YOU, ALEXANDER! FUCK YOU!!

VICTORIA MARTIN: MATH TEAM QUEEN

Kathryn Walat

Comic
Peter, late teens

Peter is the captain of his high school's Math Team, which hereto-fore has been all-male. In this direct address to the audience Peter tells why the team is going to be better because a girl named Victoria has joined it.

PETER: In case you need to review the facts. Number one: As unofficial Math Team captain and the senior on the team, I am the most mature member of the team. Number two: This is my *last chance* ever — *ever* — to prove our awesome collective mathematical brainpower at States!!!

(He collects himself, like the mature leader he is.)

Number three. As the leader of the Team, I have to accept this problem's given: We are without Sanjay Patel. And without Sanjay Patel, there is *no way* we're going to make it to States. And without one last chance for Math Team glory? High school for me is *over.*

I mean, I still go to class, even though I'm smarter than all my teachers. And this isn't me being conceited — my teachers *told* my parents this, on parents' night back in October. And I'm still senior class Treasurer, and go to all the student council meetings, and of course I'll crunch the numbers so the prom doesn't have to be in the cafeteria — but who cares about the *prom?* Or the class picnic or the senior skip day — not me — but then . . .

She came. And said we couldn't take off our sneakers in the van because our feet smelled. And brought Cracker Jacks to practice, because she said they were *retro,* and then made us all give her our prizes. Except for the tattoos. Which she made us apply to our foreheads, because she said it would give us brainpower — which it *did.*

And at the meets, while she's working on her problem set, she always gets this funny look on her face, just when she *gets* a problem, and she *knows* she's got it, and I know she's got it, and we've totally got it — and that's when I think: This is awesome!

Because the Longwood High School Math Team has started to *win* again. But this time? Math Team is — different. Better. Like, it's more than just *math*.

VICTORIA MARTIN: MATH TEAM QUEEN
Kathryn Walat

Comic
Jimmy, mid-teens

> *Jimmy, a member of his high school Math Team, is also the equip-*
> *ment manager of the school's basketball team. He's conflicted, be-*
> *cause he hero-worships Scott Sumner, the team's star, but Scott's*
> *girlfriend is Victoria Martin, a girl who has recently joined the Math*
> *Team on whom he has a big crush. This is direct address to the*
> *audience.*

JIMMY: *(Jimmy stands outside the high school gym, holding an extra-large foun-*
tain soda. He talks to the audience.) OK, *this* is the big game. In case
you don't remember, every school year, there is *the game.* And this is
that game — bigger than homecoming, bigger than the Thanksgiv-
ing game or any other football thing. It's bigger than Sanjay Patel's
totally, unbelievably awesome final Math Team meet before he moved
to Arizona. Bigger than any of the Chess Team matches — I know,
I'm on the team — bigger than the swim meet when Bruce Owen
was standing on the starting block with a total boner — *bigger* than
Bruce Owens' boner — this is the basketball State Championship
game. And we were in it. And I was even doing the stats. And Scott
Sumner — even though he is only a *junior* and no one even *knew*
his name last year — is totally, totally awesome.

And really nice to me too. Like, whenever Scott Sumner sees me,
he says: Hey Jimmy. And he means me. And he *really* means it. And
that makes me feel like when my mom wakes me up on Sunday morning sometimes — like she did this morning, because it was a big day
because I was going to do the stats for the big game — and says: Guess
who's getting blueberry muffins with maple syrup? And she means
me.

The guys on the team were so nervous in the locker room that some of them started praying. And the cheerleaders were so nervous that someone said they were all throwing up in the girls' locker room. And the whole team shaved their heads. Even second-string. But I think some of them wished they didn't now, like one of the point guards, who has really bad acne in his hairline, except now there's no hairline, so it's just a line of zits.

And the cheerleaders were all going to get their legs waxed. I don't really know why they'd do that, but I guess it's something that hurts, and the second-string forward said he thought that showed solidarity. Well, he didn't use that word, solidarity, but I was listening to the whole conversation, sitting there at my little card table next to the bench, and I know that's what he meant.

Victoria Martin is sitting in the stands right in the middle of our section, right were she always sits. She looks so *beautiful.* And when Scott Sumner runs in right at the front of the tunnel run, while they play that music that makes everyone get up and shake their butts — he always looks up to the stands, right to that spot, and I know he's looking for her. And their eyes meet. And every game I think: Wow, that's love.

OK, halftime's almost over. I really, really hope that I can make it through the second half without having to pee again, because I don't want to miss a *second* of this game.

(Jimmy runs into the game.)

THE WINNING STREAK
Lee Blessing

Dramatic
Ry, thirties

*Ry is talking to his father Omar, a retired baseball umpire whom
he has never met until just recently. He was the product of a one-
night stand Omar had long ago. Here he is trying to find some way
to connect with Omar.*

RY: You're dirty; I'll make you clean. I have an infinite supply of tiny
brushes, dental tools, tweezers so small they could hold a moth's heart
while it's still beating. An endless array of magnifying glasses which
insure that nothing, no matter how small, can ever be insignificant.
Special lights and rays that reveal, when I wear the magic glasses, what
otherwise could never be seen: paint-overs, first decisions, revisions.
I have chemicals, mysterious liquids which hold and bond and clean
and dissolve. I have a set of procedures designed to keep me from
doing harm. Because harm, once done, cannot always be undone.
Most of all, I have the humility of a scientist — the readiness to let
the artist's satyr be nothing but himself.

. . . Know what I love about my job? The colors. We think old
things are dull; we can't help it. But I can take my satyr and care-
fully apply the chemicals, strip layer after layer, until all the dirt is
gone, the humiliations at the hands of shrieking kids have disap-
peared. And then the skin shows through. And the light under the
skin. There are times the light is so bright that no one would believe
it. I've actually been asked not to restore a color completely, because
it looks too new.

. . . I understand. The paintings are old — that's how we think
of them. Why should we grant them the exuberance of our own
world? The brightest colors are always reserved for now. *(After a beat.)*
So. It stays my secret, sometimes. That last degree of vividness, the
light that could, if freed, emanate from a satyr's poisoned soul.